GLOBAL
BRAND POWER

**Available in the
Wharton Executive Essentials Series**

*Customer Centricity:
Focus on the Right Customers for Strategic Advantage,*
by Peter Fader

*Financial Literacy for Managers:
Finance and Accounting for Better Decision-Making,*
by Richard A. Lambert

*Global Brand Power:
Leveraging Branding for Long-Term Growth*
by Barbara E. Kahn

*Innovation Prowess:
Leadership Strategies for Accelerating Growth*
by George S. Day

For more information,
visit *wsp.wharton.upenn.edu*

BARBARA E. KAHN

GLOBAL BRAND POWER

Leveraging Branding for Long-Term Growth

WHARTON
SCHOOL
PRESS

Philadelphia

Published by Wharton School Press
The Wharton School
University of Pennsylvania
3620 Locust Walk
2000 Steinberg Hall-Dietrich Hall
Philadelphia, PA 19104

Email: whartonschoolpress@wharton.upenn.edu
Website: wsp.wharton.upenn.edu

Ebook ISBN: 978-1-61363-025-9
Paperback ISBN: 978-1-61363-026-6

9 8 7 6 5 4 3 2

Contents

Introduction 1

CHAPTER 1
A Brand's Role in the Four Stages of the Purchase Process 9

CHAPTER 2
Experiential Positioning of a Brand 29

CHAPTER 3
Qualitative Measurement of Brand Value 45

CHAPTER 4
Quantitative Methods for Assessing Brand Value 61

CHAPTER 5
Management of Brands 79

CHAPTER 6
Effective Brand Communications and Repositioning Strategies........ 95

Conclusion 109

Resources 113

Index 115

About the Author 121

About the Wharton Executive Essentials Series 123

Introduction

Brands today must be *global*. They must offer value across different countries and diverse cultures: that is, they must be porous enough to allow for reasonable brand and product-line extensions, broad enough to change with dynamic market conditions, consistent enough so that consumers who travel physically or virtually won't be confused, and precise enough to provide clear differentiation from the competition.

In this age of total transparency—one slipup can go around the world via social media instantaneously—a strong global brand must express the same core meanings regardless of the market it is in. If those core meanings are not stable across markets, the authenticity of the brand is threatened. Consumers who travel virtually or physically will be confused, and the brand will lose its power. If a brand is inconsistent in its central values, consumers will surely point out the discrepancies, and if they start doing this, the bottom line will suffer.

But brands and products are not the same thing. While brands must be global, products introduced to new markets should be implemented with a clear understanding of the local culture and conventions, and advertised, distributed, and priced with local market conditions in mind.

The distinction between brands and products became clear in 1985. Brands had existed before then, of course, but neither customers nor marketing managers genuinely understood their true power or realized that they had a life of their own independent from the products' attributes.

Almost without exception, pre-1985 brands were product focused. Think Coca-Cola, Gillette, Nabisco, Campbell, Lipton, Goodyear, and Kellogg. Each one of these was—and still is—a very, very strong brand, but each one also, at least initially, was identified with specific product attributes, which limited growth potential and global credibility. Other very strong brands that were developed before 1985, such as Oldsmobile and Kodak, became so closely associated with specific product characteristics that in spite of worldwide brand awareness, they offered little hope of future market success.

Before 1985, consumers were willing to pay a price premium for certain brands, but they rarely identified so closely with a brand that they would protest passionately if aspects of the brand marketing changed in a way they didn't like. Similarly, marketers were well aware of brands, but they didn't know how to build them, leverage them appropriately, or encourage consumers to establish relationships with them.

So what happened in 1985 to change all of this? That was the year the Coca-Cola Company introduced New Coke and removed what the company subsequently called Classic Coke from store shelves.

There were good market reasons for developing the new product. Coca-Cola was a much bigger global company than Pepsi Cola, thanks to Coke's global expansion and domination of the restaurant and vending machine markets. However, the market share of Coca-Cola was lagging in supermarkets, the only channel where consumers could choose for themselves. Pepsi Cola had launched the "Pepsi Challenge" advertising campaign, which suggested that consumers preferred the taste of Pepsi to that of Coke. In response, after significant market testing, Coca-Cola launched New Coke, which had a product taste that consumers seemed to prefer in blind taste tests.

What Coca-Cola executives did not realize at the time was that consumers were not making soft drink choices based on critical product attributes such as taste but instead were choosing products because of their loyalty to the brand. For years, the Coca-Cola brand was associated with small-town Americana. Coke was featured in Norman Rockwell ads, in World War II "Support Our Troops" campaigns, and in Christmas time celebrations. Coca-Cola traveled the world with the US Olympic team. The quintessential American TV family—Ozzie, Harriet, David, and Ricky Nelson—drank Coke. Coca-Cola was "the real thing." Coke was "it." When Coca-Cola executives removed Classic Coke from the shelves, they removed more than a product; they took away something dear to their customers' hearts. Subsequent market research revealed that consumers felt betrayed. "I couldn't be more upset if my husband cheated on me," one customer complained.

This shocking reaction proved to Coca-Cola and the world that consumers were loyal to brands in and of themselves, and not necessarily to product features. This realization radically changed the way both academics and business practitioners thought about brands. Now, more than 25 years later, we have amassed significant knowledge about how branding works. Marketing managers understand that brands are an investment; they have value in and of themselves, over and above the tangible capital invested.

With this new knowledge, managers have been able to create cohesive long-term global-brand strategies that can provide substantial growth opportunities for a firm. Strong brands have higher market share, higher prices, and higher margins. Since 1985, the growth of the top 100 brands has exceeded the growth of the advanced economy GDP by more than 35%.

Consumers have responded as well. Although there were strong brands prior to 1985, new marketing strategies of well-executed brands have created even more powerful loyalties. A new generation of consumers no longer thinks it odd to self-identify with a brand. Consumers proudly wear brand logos.

Brands are mentioned often in popular TV shows, songs, and books because they quickly establish character dimensionality. And when Steve Jobs—a consummate marketer who understood the new global love affair with brands—passed away, consumers responded by placing flowers at the appropriate altar, the Apple stores. Brands have truly become a religious experience.

This growth in the power of global brands is not by chance. We have learned how to build such brands, how to position them appropriately, how to create emotional bonds, and how to continually reposition these brands to keep pace with changing market dynamics. We have also learned how to measure these emotional and symbolic associations and account for the economic value of brands and the price premiums branded goods can enjoy. Bottom line: We now know how to leverage and manage brands to help the firm grow.

Good brands are not accidents. Their long-term value to the firm has to be developed and managed over time. The best brands form relationships with their customers. In doing so, brand meanings may also be co-created through social media communities and customer-engagement strategies. Grappling with all these issues is the challenge that every marketer faces.

Moving from Product-Focused to Customer-Focused Brands

To understand how branding strategies have changed, we need to look at the basic mechanics of a market. In the simplest terms, a market is an exchange between buyers and sellers. If you think of the extremes of the continuum, you can have a seller's market, in which the seller has all the power, or a buyer's market, where the buyer has ultimate choice and therefore the market power. Obviously, branding strategies should differ as a function of the nature of the market.

In a seller's market, if customers want your product, they come to you. In this case, it makes sense for brands to focus on product attributes. Growth strategies come from developing new products based on shared product experience or selling products that you produce to new markets. When Coca-Cola developed a new diet soft drink and branded it Diet Coke, it became an instant success because customers understood that the new product would have attributes (cola flavor) similar to those of the core product.

Most markets today, though, do not favor the seller. Because of globalization, deregulation, threats of substitutes, and increased competition, markets have become very competitive, and buyers have a great deal of choice. In this situation, persuading a buyer to purchase from you rather than from the competition means focusing on what customers want and offering something that they value.

All customers are not the same, which means trying to satisfy all customers is futile. A buyer's market necessitates segmentation strategies. Segmentation is a process by which a firm partitions the market into submarkets such that customers' responses to marketing variables within the submarkets are similar, and responses across submarkets vary greatly. In this situation, marketers pick an attractive segment to target, and brands must foster an emotional, authentic connection with the targeted customers. Brands need to engender trust and reliability while generating strong loyalty. In today's connected world, customers find out about products from not only the firms that produce them but also other customers. Thus, brands need to engender strong emotional customer-focused bonds that motivate consumers to build relationships with them and to form social communities around them. Profitability comes from premium or value-pricing strategies, long-term relationships with the customer, and cross-selling.

Customers Own the Brand

Reverence for the Apple brand proves just how deep consumer loyalty can run. Such loyalty exists beyond consumer markets. Many IT specialists are very faithful to IBM; OEMs respect Intel chips; logistics officers commit to FedEx. While customers do respond to marketing messages from a company, they also form impressions based on their own experiences. Gap learned this the hard way when it tried to introduce a new Gap logo. The logo lasted just one week before consumers revolted and forced Gap back to the original design.

When customers form a strong relationship with a brand, they can also be the best advocates for it. Many consumers self-identify as Starbucks aficionados or Dunkin' drinkers. The loyalty to one chain or another can be as strong as loyalty to a sports team. If a brand strategy really resonates with consumers, those consumers will pitch that coveted product to friends and beyond. However, consumers can also use a bad experience to punish a brand or use the brand's fame to bring attention to their own cause. For example, PETA frequently starts campaigns against well-known brands because it knows those stories are more likely to be covered by the mainstream media.

Understanding Brand Equity

All of us can identify good brands after they have succeeded. We can also identify colossal failures. But how does anyone know the difference before the marketplace reveals the answer? That is the goal of this book: to help managers build, measure, and manage strong brands.

The topics I will cover include the following:

- Since customers own the brand, it is essential to understand the underlying processes that customers use to evaluate the brands. What implications do these psychological processes have for designing brands? What is the role of social media in creating customer-centric brands?

- Strong brands are better positioned than competitive brands. What are the mechanisms that best position a brand? How is a total brand experience built, taking into account not only the cognitive associations with brands, but also the social, behavioral, emotional, and cultural associations?

- Measurement is necessary to understand what brands mean and how they can be used to add value to a firm.

  o We will discuss the most widely used qualitative brand measurement techniques: laddering, ZMET, and ethnography.

  o We will discuss the most widely used quantitative brand measurement techniques (including measuring brand awareness, brand attitudes, brand emotions, and brand relationships and satisfaction) and the two most widely used commercial global branding measurement techniques: BrandAsset Valuator and Interbrand brand value model.

- We will explore how brands can work as a system to create value. What is a house of brands versus a branded house? What role does a brand play in corporate social responsibility strategies? How are branding strategies affected by mergers and acquisitions that require the blending of brands? How can brand extensions, co-branding, and licensing help achieve growth?

- We will look at how to ensure that brands stay relevant. What are the best ways to reposition a brand once it has lost its way? How should brands respond to brand crises?

I will combine the leading-edge knowledge that has been developed by academics and strategic brand managers over the past 25 years—including most notably what brands have learned from actual marketplace experiences—to get at the core of what makes a great brand strategy. I will also show why great brands matter. Strong brands are more than easily and globally recognizable; they are also well positioned to make a sizable return on investment. Indeed, few other marketing strategies can so dependably deliver to the bottom line.

Chapter 1

A Brand's Role in the Four Stages of the Purchase Process

In this chapter:

- Living Stage: Awareness of a Need
- Planning Stage: Creation of Interest About Considered Brands
- Shopping Stage: Desire for the Right Branded Product
- Experiencing Stage: Purchase and Repurchase
- Stirring the Soup at Campbell

S hopping for mustard used to be such a simple experience, or so it seemed. Jar or squeeze bottle? French's? Heinz? Or Grey Poupon? Throw in a couple of regional favorites, and that was pretty much the universe from which most mustard consumers made their selection.

Advertising had an influence on the actual choice, as did a host of other factors. Did you want the mustard that the two guys in the Rolls-Royces were sharing? Then buy Grey Poupon. Or did you want a mustard that was sure to call to mind ballparks and Fourth of July picnics? That would be French's. But choice was limited, and sales venues were predictable.

No more. Google the phrase "best mustards," and seriouseats.com will give you taste-test results on 39 mustards in six broad categories: best yellow, best Dijon, best deli-style and spicy brown, best honey, best full of seeds, and best "other" (including "most sinus clearing"). There are six-sided jars and organics to choose among, and store brands (Trader Joe's and Whole Foods 365) that are more meaningful to some consumers than the traditional brands. This array of mustards, it seems, is just one mundane example of a world awash in choice.

Since time immemorial, people have been turning into customers when they've decided they had a need or a desire that could be satisfied by making a purchase, but today the process is no longer a simple "to buy or not to buy" decision. A strong brand has multiple opportunities along a customer's path to purchase to influence the final selection and create ultimate loyalty. This purchase process can be quite nuanced but is characterized by four main stages: living, planning, shopping, and experiencing.

Figure 1.1
Critical Stages of the Customer Purchase Process

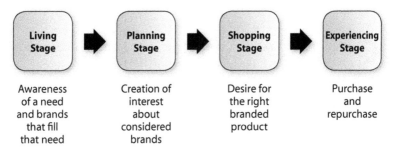

Living Stage	Planning Stage	Shopping Stage	Experiencing Stage
Awareness of a need and brands that fill that need	Creation of interest about considered brands	Desire for the right branded product	Purchase and repurchase

When your brand is not the one purchased, you have to figure out at what stage it fell out of consideration. Consumers may not buy your brand because they never heard of it or because they have a misguided view of it. They may reject it because it is out of stock or wrongly priced—or because your competition has a better brand message, a problem addressed in the next chapter. Complicating matters further, any one of these stages can occur either online, offline, or on a mobile phone, and can be made alone or influenced by others in person or virtually. In addition, customers can react automatically, with little thought and attention; or they might react in a more controlled fashion, with greater cognitive elaboration and attention.

Strong brands frequently have significant advantages at every stage, but having an advantage at an early stage does not necessarily mean the customer will end up purchasing your brand. One particularly frustrating example of this, called showrooming, has been plaguing Best Buy.

Showrooming is a process in which a customer conducts the planning or pre-purchase stage offline in a brick-and-mortar store (such as Best Buy) and then makes the purchase online at a site such as Amazon. Similarly, customers might choose to learn about the advantages and disadvantages of a branded product from a company website and then buy a knockoff somewhere else.

If a company can come to understand the psychological processes a consumer goes through during each stage of the buying decision it will help increase the likelihood that consumers will develop a long-term relationship with that brand.

Living Stage: Awareness of a Need

Consumers are people first, spending most of their time wrapped up in the daily details of life. The key goal for a brand, then, is to be relevant and noticed. Brands become relevant when consumers decide they have a need or desire that can be satisfied by a purchase. Sometimes this desire is triggered by a natural occurrence: Someone is hungry and decides to buy something to eat. Or the toaster breaks and has to be replaced. Sometimes the desire is triggered by the marketplace: BMW announces its newest sports car convertible, and suddenly a "need" is identified that the customer didn't know she had. Or a new recipe is featured in the daily newspaper, creating a desire to buy the brands listed among the ingredients. Sometimes the trigger is what other people are doing. Dwyane Wade of the Miami Heat starts wearing lens-free glasses, and they become de rigueur for a night out on South Beach. Or needs can be triggered by a change in life status: People get married, they move, children are born, and all sorts of purchases must be made.

Brands themselves can trigger a need

Even when life's circumstances don't initiate the purchase process, brands themselves can trigger it. Apple has been very successful in associating its brand with innovations that create needs that consumers did not know they had. Before the iPad existed, most people did not know their lives were incomplete without an e-tablet, let alone an iPad 3. FedEx created the need for the overnight delivery of letters and important documents before lawyers and accountants even anticipated the urgency.

Brands can also spark desires through product-line extensions. Snapple and Ben & Jerry's ice cream came up with exotic flavors that encouraged consumers to seek variety in their choices, which frequently led to higher consumption. Hill's Science Diet pet food similarly created the need for diet and healthy food for dogs and cats. Brands can create desires through advertising in traditional media or via online reminders, emails, and flash sales sites such as Gilt.com, RueLaLa.com, and Fab. com. Even if the brands themselves don't spark the need, they can be in the right place at the right time when the need pops up. AT&T promotes services through listing its phone number in free mover guides distributed by the US Postal Service.

Strong global brands have high awareness

Once the need or desire for a product or service is established through either natural events or marketing activity, brands must capture the customer's attention in order to be considered. Here, strong global brands hold a critical advantage—they are already in the consumers' consideration set, which usually consists of only three to four brands for a specific product class. Strong brands also come to mind quickly. They have multiple connections in consumers' memories, and this gives them a memory-encoding advantage. The more links a brand has, the easier that brand is to recall when a need occurs. Weak brands can be stored under a general product category, and thus are recalled as products (e.g., basketball shoes) rather than as a brand (e.g., Nike or Adidas).

For obvious reasons, brands strive to be top of mind at the right time and the right place, but how does a brand create high awareness? In fact, it can be a bit tautological. Strong brands have large market share and extensive distribution, and this creates high top-of-mind awareness. High top-of-mind awareness allows for easy recall in many different circumstances, encouraging consideration and purchase, and further strengthening the brand.

For newcomers, high brand awareness can be built through advertising, word-of-mouth or viral strategies, or public relations campaigns (or stunts!), but even the best advertising strategies are ineffective if consumers do not pay attention. The message has to cut through the clutter.

Brands must grab customers' attention

Focusing attention—the processing activity that a consumer devotes to a particular stimulus—can come about in two ways: voluntarily and involuntarily.

Voluntary attention refers to when a consumer is actively taking in information about the brand—but this creates several hurdles. First, voluntary attention is shaped by a consumer's perspective. The consumer pays attention only to stimuli to which he has been exposed. If consumers don't visit your web page or go to the store where your brand is distributed, they will not see your brand. If the consumer is shopping only within a specific price range, and your brand does not fall into that range, again, the consumer will not notice your brand. Thus, even if consumers are willing to pay attention to information about your brand, they have to be exposed to it. And exposure is biased by preconceived perceptions and expectations. This again points to the catch-22 advantage that strong brands enjoy—they are often the only brands consumers notice.

The second problem with voluntary attention is that even if consumers have the opportunity to process information about your brand, they must have the incentive and capacity to do so. How do you increase the likelihood that they will process information about your brand? Make the message enjoyable, funny, surprising, and aesthetically pleasing. Put the information in the right place at the right time. Enlist your consumers' friends to carry the message for you. This is the appeal and potential of social media sites such as Facebook and Pinterest. If friends like or pin your brand, potential consumers will more likely be motivated and will have the opportunity to pay attention to your message.

Involuntary attention refers to when a consumer's attention is grabbed by something he didn't anticipate even noticing, such as loud noises, novel images, or unexpected copy. Factors that contrast (rather than assimilate) in size, color, position, and distinctiveness tend to be more effective. Humor also works. Consumers have a natural need for closure, so incomplete figures and images can attract attention. Attention can wane, however, as consumers adapt to the stimuli. Food that is at first exciting and interesting often grows mundane with repeated exposure. Similarly, marketing stimuli have to be kept fresh, or consumers will adapt and not actively notice them anymore.

One easy way to grab attention is through sexual antics. "Sex sells" is an adage even grade-school students know. But nudity and sex can backfire and cause no end of trouble. Famously, Calvin Klein used underage sexy female models to sell jeans, and although the advertising definitely got attention, it drew massive criticism, forcing the company to withdraw the ads. Abercrombie & Fitch increased visitors to its stores by featuring sexy models in catalogs and in stores, but some of this advertising also went too far, again causing a backlash.

Recently, online retailer Zappos has been featuring naked models (with strategically placed censor bars) engaging in routine outdoor activities such as jogging or riding a scooter. The ads, with the tagline "To help you break a sweat without breaking the law," are designed to call attention to Zappos's new focus on clothing. The campaign, which includes digital advertising as well as print with QR codes, features the shapes and curves of many different body types. If the consumer clicks on the QR code, he is taken to the Zappos mobile site, where he can watch videos or select outfits for the model to wear. Of course, if so inclined, he can also buy the items using his smartphone.

Planning Stage: Creation of Interest About Considered Brands

As difficult as it is to draw attention for your brand, it is even harder to get someone to seriously consider purchasing it. At a local supermarket, I once counted more than 50 soft drink brands on the shelf. That an average consumer could name perhaps 12 of them without looking at the shelf illustrates the shrinkage that occurs from poor brand awareness. But even among those dozen, the average shopper will consider purchasing at most three or four. Which three or four are considered (out of the original 50) is a matter of managing the information that consumers receive about your brand over time. How does the consumer filter your brand messaging? How much searching is she willing to do? How is this information processed and through what lens? Finally, what is the ability of your brand to be remembered clearly, positively, and uniquely?

Attention is not enough; people have to "get it." A brand needs attention to have power, but that is only a start. Consumers must both notice the brand and understand its messaging. If consumers are faced with too much information, they will likely block all of it out. Additionally, consumers must have the ability to process the information. That will happen only if the information is simple enough to understand and if consumers have enough time to process it. JCPenney recently tried to rebrand its stores with a new "fair and square" pricing strategy. Consumers did pay attention, but they didn't understand what the new strategy was, and same-store sales fell nearly 20%.

A more successful way of sparking interest is to recast the product. To return to a brand mentioned at the start of this chapter, French's mustard, made by Reckitt Benckiser, has been seen as a tasty topping for hot dogs, hamburgers, and sandwiches for more than a hundred years. But French's wanted to find new uses and new users, so it recast its mustard as a spicy ingredient in gourmet recipes. An advertising campaign featured French's mustard as the key ingredient in a salmon entrée served with a glass of wine. The image changes not only the interest in the brand, from a condiment to an ingredient, but also the context, from ballpark to elegant dinner party. The campaign has been supplemented with a Facebook page that each day highlights new recipes calling for mustard.

Customers' memory for brands is shaped by expectations

Whether consumers will consider your brand (if they have not considered it before) is a function of whether they are willing to search for information. In general, the amount of search is a function of an intuitive cost-benefit analysis. If a perceived benefit exists for taking the time and trouble to search for information, consumers will; if not, they "satisfice"—or stop at "good enough."

In frequently purchased categories such as toothpaste, toilet tissue, or dishwashing liquid—especially where the cost of a wrong choice is small—consumers frequently do not search much at all. Instead they rely on preconceived expectations of the category and of the brands they know. If circumstances change, perhaps due to stock-outs or price changes, consumers may be willing to search more. When something enters the market, either a brand or a feature, consumers may then be willing to search. In less frequently purchased categories, where preconceived expectations do not exist, consumers will generally search more extensively before making a purchase. In any event, this newly collected information will not be interpreted in a vacuum but rather alongside existing expectations. Information that is different from what a consumer expects is more diagnostic, and negative information is more salient than positive information. Consumers tend to recall very salient attributes, rather than making nuanced judgments. That said, consumers are not looking for disconfirming evidence; they are instead subject to what is known as confirmation bias. They take in information that supports or confirms what they already think they know, and tend to ignore or reject information that runs counter to preconceived ideas. This makes it difficult for brand managers to change preconceived ideas.

But there is good news for brands that in the past might not have been able to penetrate consumer apathy or negativity: People will respond to the opinions of their friends and other personal influencers. Today, social media outlets such as Facebook and Twitter provide a forum for friends to weigh in. Through online relationships, current loyal customers can possibly persuade new customers to jump on the brandwagon.

Brand schemas are sets of brand associations in memory

Every brand, weak or strong, has an identifiable set of associations stored in a consumer's long-term memory. This brand schema is a knowledge structure, or a network of thoughts and memories associated with the brand. Information such as the brand name and characteristics, evaluative reaction to the brand, and its marketing is stored in nodes connected by associative links. Strong brands have better developed consumer knowledge structures than weak ones.

This knowledge structure in memory is also called a semantic associative network, or words about the brand that are linked in memory. When something activates one node in the network, an impulse spreads and activates other nodes. Some of the links are strong because they have been well rehearsed; others are weaker. The level of abstraction varies as well. Some links are concrete (such as functional or performance attributes), others are more abstract (such as personality traits or experiential values). Some of the links are more unique to the brand; others, more common to the product category. Links might be positive, negative, autobiographical, or just neutral. The complete associative network, or schema, is the total package of links that are brought to mind when a brand is evoked and represents the full set of expectations a person has about that brand.

For example, a schema for the brand McDonald's might include yellow arches, Ronald McDonald, hamburgers, fast food, french fries, family, and the place I go to after school. Each of these associations may trigger another set of associations that are further away from the brand's core meaning. For example, the family as an association might be linked to other family-friendly activities. One can think of these brand schemas almost as streams of consciousness that start with the brand as the anchor. These schemas are often drawn as diagrams, with the brand at the center and the associations as networked links attached to it, with the stronger links closer to the brand and the weaker links farther from the center.

When new information is collected about a brand, it is evaluated through this existing brand schema. If the new information is congruent with the schema, it is usually accepted, and the brand schema, or image, is further developed. But if the new information is incongruent with the existing brand schema, it is likely to be rejected. These schemas are thus critical for a brand manager to understand because, in essence, they suggest exactly what the consumer is willing to accept about the brand. As we'll see in chapter 5, brand schemas also form the foundation for just how far the brand can be stretched to allow for new growth. For example, as suggested by the schema just mentioned, consumers might have trouble associating healthy snacks with McDonald's even if, in fact, its menu items can be shown to be more nutritious than some alternatives. This is a thorny problem that McDonald's has had to face as it tried to respond to public scrutiny about the health aspects of its food.

Strong brands have clear images

Strong brands have better-developed consumer knowledge structures, and the links are uniquely associated with the brand. Google, Coca-Cola, Macy's, Visa, and Ikea are all clearly differentiated bands, and consumers have extensive experience with them. For weaker brands, the associations may be stored under the product category and not with the specific brand. Think American Airlines, *TV Guide*, or Kleenex. All three have lost their clear brand structure and are now associated more generically with the product category.

Whatever mix of promotional vehicles is employed, to keep a brand strong, the image must be consistent at every consumer touch point. The image can be functional or performance related, or abstract and metaphoric. Finally, strong brands clearly and easily present themselves to consumers with no contradictory, confusing, or excessive information.

Shopping Stage: Desire for the Right Branded Product

When consumers are deciding which brand to ultimately choose, they frequently make price-quality inferences: Is the price I am paying worth the quality I am getting? These types of trade-offs are very difficult, even for an experienced shopper. Further, customers' preferences are not fixed and are often constructed on the fly as a function of the choice context. Even if consumers can accurately judge their own tastes in the moment, they may have difficulty forecasting future preferences if, as is often the case, the purchase and consumption are not simultaneous.

When consumers lack the time or expertise to analyze the trade-offs in detail, they tend to fall back on a peripheral cue, or they rely on heuristics or decision shortcuts. In these situations, brands that have very strong images and that inspire confidence and credibility often become the default selection. Rather than carefully inspecting the garment and looking at the craftsmanship, consumers may judge it holistically and decide that the luxury brand, say Burberry or Louis Vuitton, ensures high quality. This process is especially operant when quality is ambiguous or when the choice seems risky. Insurance companies and banks spend a lot of money marketing their brands for this reason. Furthermore, if a customer feels accountable for his or her choice, a strong brand name can help justify the decision.

Emotional reactions to brands

Consumers may also choose a brand from a consideration set if they feel strong emotions toward it, even if they cannot rationally justify these emotions. Strong brands generate feelings of warmth, fun, or excitement, along with feelings of security and social approval. We know that emotional ties to brands are especially compelling in predicting choice. That's why so much consumer advertising, whether in traditional media or in social media venues, is generated to produce powerful emotional reactions to a brand.

Ownership of strong brands can also confer status. This is particularly the case in the world's largest emergent market, China. The need there to show status traces back to the Cultural

Revolution of the 1960s and '70s, when Mao suits produced coherence through sameness but hierarchy through detail. One could instantly identify someone's place in the hierarchy by the number of pockets (four, two, or none) on his Mao suit. Similarly, carrying a luxury Louis Vuitton purse now indicates one's place in a status hierarchy. China is already the second-largest luxury market in the world, after Japan, and is expected to claim the top spot by 2020.

The critical role of trust

In addition to reacting emotionally to brands, consumers typically need to trust a brand in order to buy one of its products. A recent study by BAV Consulting, a group that is running one of the largest studies of brands in the world and is a unit of the WPP Group, has found that trust has become even more important since the 2008 global recession. At the turn of the present century, surveys showed that people trusted almost half of all brands. By 2009, that number had been nearly halved, from 49% to 25%. Bank, insurance, and financial services brands have been particularly hard hit, but trust has declined across all industries. Prior to 2008, trust was one of the most important, but also one of the least differentiating, of the 48 BAV imagery attributes. With the decline in trust overall, in the words of BAV, trust is now "the new black," the great differentiator.

The BAV data also show that one of the main drivers of the trustworthiness of brands since 2009 is recommendation from customers. Traditional broadcast messaging that emanates from the brand is far less effective at establishing trust than an endorsement from a social media friend. Putting a Facebook tag on your message indicates that you are willing to have others in the social media world discuss your brand and message, and this conveys implicit transparency and inspires a social contract. Thus, the Facebook or Twitter tag becomes a badge that appears to both ensure and symbolize trust.

Presumably, a dishonest brand could not stand up to scrutiny in the social media world. As with everything in the branding universe, trust also must continue to be earned. There is evidence in the BAV database that the increasing arrogance, if continued unbridled, of the Apple, Facebook, and Google brands could threaten their ultimate trustworthiness. Companies should not be focusing on the specific social media brands of the moment, but rather on the role of recommendations and social influence as predictor of trust in the brand. In BAV terms, companies should think of "social as a business model."

Experiencing Stage: Purchase and Repurchase

Strong brands are the ones that consumers remain loyal to over time, and the strongest are those that customers form a relationship with and become advocates for. Apple is such a brand. Its customers not only exhibit fierce, almost religious loyalty, but also feel the need to convert others. Consumers who have strong relationships with brands are willing to participate in chat room discussions and engage in Facebook or Twitter activities with their brands. In the next chapter, we talk about how a company can help create these strong relationships by delivering a differentiating brand experience. Here we focus on the customer's point of view.

Customers' relationships with brands

Relationships with brands go well beyond purchase or repurchase transactions. From the customer's point of view, the pre-consumption, consumption, and post-consumption occasions matter as well. Relationships with brands, like personal relationships, are built over time through a series of positive experiences. Here, more is not necessarily better; what counts are meaningful interactions.

When consumers become completely involved with a brand, they may form what is called a brand community. As researchers at the University of Illinois, Thomas O'Guinn and Albert Muñiz identified three defining factors of such communities: a shared consciousness of kind, the presence of shared rituals and traditions, and a shared sense of moral responsibility. For a model, look at Harley-Davidson. It reaps many benefits from grassroots activities that are dedicated to a perceived lifestyle based on its brand.

Fundamental to this kind of loyalty is the idea that customers buy into the brand's authentic philosophy and values. Brands with a higher purpose to their mission engender customer commitment. Consider Warby Parker, the online eyeglass company that gives away a pair of glasses for every pair it sells.

Another way to increase brand stickiness is through gamification. Interesting games around a brand can create topics of conversation, social currency, and brand affinity. For example, Green Giant, a food company owned by General Mills, teamed up with FarmVille (a Zynga online game) to capitalize on consumers' manic attachment to the game. Special labels on Green Giant Fresh products come with stickers allowing consumers to receive free Farm Cash. Tabasco created a game for Facebook called Pass the Tabasco, in which customers earn points by uploading their videos showing how they use Tabasco on food.

The ubiquity of mobile technology and online interaction provides countless mechanisms for customers to engage with the brand and to socialize around it. And this counts for a lot: Engaged consumers exhibit greater loyalty, connection, emotional resonance, and trust. To this end, brands should respond to comments or complaints that are aired in public or on social media forums.

Southwest Airlines has several full-time employees dedicated to monitoring online and social media activity about its brand, and uses some outside partners as well. Although numbers change quickly, at one point the airline had 12 million monthly visitors to its web page, 1 million Twitter followers, and 1.3 million Facebook "likes." Southwest tries to provide meaningful content to travel bloggers, avid travelers, and brand fanatics, and encourages employees to contribute content as well. The airline also strives to personalize the interactions and to respond to as many customers as possible, especially when a customer has a problem or a question. All this activity builds a personal bond between Southwest and its loyal fliers.

Customer relationship management strategies that result in continuous, relevant, and personalized communications between the brand and the customer improve customer retention and profitability, build loyalty, *and* increase share of wallet. Targeting the right customer with the right offer at the right time through the right channel (which requires significant data analyses capabilities) both increases ROI and strengthens brand equity. As we will discuss in chapter 5, this increased brand equity can then be a platform for significant growth.

Credit or blame after the purchase

Studies have shown that most customers do not complain after purchasing a product. For those who do complain, however, 95% are placated by a satisfactory response and ultimately repurchase the brand. Even when the response is unsatisfactory, 30% repurchase, as long as the firm doesn't ignore the complaint. The speed of response also makes a difference. Quickly resolving the problem, especially if it is a minor problem, results in strong loyalty in the future. The moral: Even if you don't have a comforting response, be quick to acknowledge the customer's problem.

Stirring the Soup at Campbell

Campbell Soup Company, a manufacturer and marketer of branded convenience food products with almost $7.7 billion in net sales, has operations in multiple nations around the world. Campbell features products that focus on simple meals, baked snacks, and healthy beverages. Its best-known brands are the ones for which the company is named, the ones that Andy Warhol immortalized with his famous painting of a Campbell's tomato soup can. But even historic, iconic brands can lose consumers' affection and fall out of favor. To stay relevant and contemporary, Campbell recognized that it had to reinsert its brand meaningfully in consumers' lives. Using a strategy based on the staged decision process described earlier, Campbell rebuilt brand equity by reaching out to consumers both at home and in the store.

Targeting the living stage of the purchase process, Campbell recognized that homemakers are creatures of habit and that most households have a repertoire of 11–15 menus they continuously cycle through. Campbell had a clear interest in bringing new customers to its brand, so it looked for ways to get homemakers first to consider cooking something different, and then to consider specific new recipes that included Campbell products as ingredients.

Company executives learned that their message needed to feed into the consumer's mind-set, yet that mind-set could change depending on a consumer's location. When consumers plan a new meal at home, they are likely to have lofty goals, such as to make something healthy. But when they consider a new meal while in the store, they are more likely to focus on sensory aspects or price. Further complicating the appropriate messaging strategy was the realization that ideas for meals could come to mind at random times, not necessarily in the store or in the kitchen. To influence consumers at these pivotal moments,

Campbell used the Internet and email to reach the consumer outside the store and made connections through cell phones to reach the consumer within the store.

Creating the need for a new recipe, and specifically one that included soups, was only part of the battle; the company also had to make sure consumers considered its brand. While many homemakers had heard of Campbell and its brand of soups, they weren't inspired to choose what they saw as a tired and old-fashioned option, something a stay-at-home mother might serve to her family when they were sick. The lasting impression was that the Campbell brand was stuck in the past, a product more suited to flu season than to nouvelle cuisine.

Further, Campbell's soup was seen as artificial and processed, like airline food. Obviously, these were not images that Campbell relished. Campbell upgraded the product experience and embarked on an ambitious advertising and repackaging campaign to reposition the product as delicious food for young and healthy people.

As will be discussed in chapter 6, for a repositioning strategy to be effective, the consumer has to notice the transformation and believe it. To get over that hurdle, Campbell relied on extensive market research, using both qualitative and quantitative methods to determine how the company could work within its iconic packaging and brand impressions to update the imagery and make it more positive.

All this helped bring customers into the store—for the shopping stage—but here still more problems arose. The company's studies showed that consumers thought soup was the second most difficult category to shop in the grocery store. Campbell accepted the challenge. The company studied consumers' reactions using biometric techniques, and re-designed its shelf displays to make the category easier to comprehend, even with a very quick scan. After the redesign,

94% of shoppers indicated that the section was now "easy to shop," with 86% checking the top box on the ratings scale. Even with a less intimidating aisle, typically only about 50% of shoppers walk down the soup aisle. And of those who do walk down the aisle, only 50% or so make a purchase, and of course that purchase is not always Campbell's. Making your brand stand out in a supermarket aisle where shoppers are whizzing by without paying attention to most of the visual stimuli is not an easy feat. Even if shoppers are paying attention to the aisle, they do not always see what you want them to see.

Yet another complication is that many shoppers are stressed or frustrated, which makes the whole process negative. To bring more of the positive emotions back into the in-store experience, Campbell mapped facial expressions and used eye tracking to learn how shoppers actually scan a soup shelf. Through that, the company learned that shoppers are more likely to feel positive emotions when they discover something appealing or surprising on the shelf. Synthesizing all this information, Campbell implemented a radical redesign of its soup displays in the supermarket.

The jury is still out as to how successful the whole strategy will be at encouraging consumers to use more soup. Initial tests are positive. More consumers are looking for soup ingredients, the reactions to the branding campaign are more positive and emotional, and the new store displays are receiving positive reactions from the trade. Even without a final success-or-failure tally, Campbell has learned that building a relationship with consumers requires understanding the whole customer decision-making process.

The ultimate goal of a brand is to manage customer satisfaction over time. A strong, clear brand image can create expectations that will help consumers make the right decisions and establish ongoing trust. Strong brand positioning provides a reason in and of itself for the brand to be chosen. Post-purchase, brands that respond quickly to glitches and provide ongoing value for future purchases reinforce the quality of the initial decision and build solid brand-customer relationships for the future. This in turn inspires brand referral and evangelism that can establish an authentic brand community. That's Campbell's ultimate brand goal.

In the next chapter, I explore the fundamental principle of branding: creating a unique, experiential brand positioning. This is the brand's DNA and what differentiates it from any other brand. A strong global brand is one that has correctly positioned itself relative to its competition and for its core customer segment.

Chapter 2

Experiential Positioning of a Brand

In this chapter:

- Strong Global Brands Are Uniquely Positioned
- Positioning Requires Making Choices
- Positioning Requires Choosing a Relevant and Desirable Advantage
- 21st-Century Brand Positioning Is Experiential
- Going Deep with Origins

In the late 1980s, the Estée Lauder Companies set out to create a brand that would revolutionize the cosmetics industry. At the time, the world of elite department store cosmetics was glitzy and glamorous. Counters made of chrome and glass, sometimes with hints of gold, featured dramatic, colorful makeup and perfumes from global companies such as Chanel and Yves St. Laurent.

Not so with Origins. The new brand from the Estée Lauder Companies would be defiantly different. Unlike the flashy cosmetic counters, the Origins store-within-stores began using natural woods and earth tones. Moreover, the company opened independent retail outlets in malls devoted solely to Origins products.

The products were unique as well. The line included plant-based skin care, makeup, and aromatherapy products. Origins was the first cosmetics brand to develop earth and animal-friendly practices and packaging. It had a Zen-like and "EST" aura that was perfect for the times, and for a while Origins products sold well.

The 1990s, though, brought a steeper slope. Originally cast as a high-end department store line, Origins increasingly became associated in consumers' minds with fast-proliferating mall retailers such as the Body Shop and Bath & Body Works. "Green" products generally burgeoned, too, swelling the crowd trying to stand outside traditional cosmetics.

Then, in the early 2000s, the legendary talk show host Oprah Winfrey, at the peak of her popularity, revealed on air that she liked meditating in the tub with wonderful bath products and that one of her favorites was the Origins Ginger Souffle Whipped Body Crème. Given Oprah's influence in her heyday, sales of Origins Ginger bath products soared, and Ginger Souffle remains one of the top sellers over a decade later. But this emphasis on the ginger scent and bath products created an overall impression of the Origins brand as just aromatherapy, which did little justice to the whole Origins line and made it difficult to differentiate the brand from other popular aromatherapy brands of the time.

Strong Global Brands Are Uniquely Positioned

People often talk about a brand as a modern patent—which suggests that there is something unique about it that cannot be copied. And indeed, creating that unique position is one of the most important tasks in building a strong global brand. The strongest brands have very clear positioning strategies that highlight their key benefits over all others in their product category. There's no incremental positioning for these category giants. *Disruptive* positioning provides a clear differentiation between them and the also-rans, and disruptive is just what Origins sought to be.

Developing a sustainable positioning strategy requires tackling three strategic components, all of which must work together for the brand to succeed. The first involves identifying the appropriate competitive set, or the frame of reference against which the brand is compared. The second is that the brand must enjoy a key sustainable competitive differential advantage among this competitive set. Finally, the brand must be targeted to the right strategic segment. With Origins, the Estée Lauder Companies got the launch just right but failed to protect the long-term interests of its new brand.

Identifying the appropriate competitive set

Unless a product is a monopoly, every brand has competition. The consumer evaluates brands within a competitive set, in which all brands include shared characteristics and minimum requirements. For example, for consumers to consider a brand in the competitive set called "grocery stores," a retail outlet must have a produce section or it is not considered a grocery store. The label "organic food" must meet standards set and revised annually by a national board. To call oneself a "low-cost provider" won't pass muster if "low-cost" earns the scorn of social media. In some cases, membership in a category is determined by regulation. Only sparkling wines that come from a certain region in France can be called champagne.

Choosing the appropriate competitive set is critical because a brand delineates its differential advantage in comparison to the other brands in that set. With Origins, the Estée Lauder Companies identified luxury department store cosmetics as the brand's competitive set, and consumers accepted that. But with Oprah's endorsement and the brand's profile, which included stand-alone mall stores, Origins' reference-set identity became blurred. Was it a high-end department store brand? A specialty retail brand targeted to a niche need? And could it be both at the same time?

Offering a sustainable competitive differential advantage

In addition to being a player in the appropriate competitive set, a strong brand must also offer something special that no other brand in that set can duplicate. Figuring out what this point of differentiation is can be tricky, but three questions can help solve the problem.

1. What do you do better than anyone else? But to answer that question strategically, you have to answer two further questions.
2. Is this thing that you do better than anyone else important to your target segment?
3. To whom are you comparing yourself?

Your product might well offer multiple potential advantages, but the one to feature in a strong positioning statement should take into account the answers to all three questions. In fact, seeing how these components fit together can explain how the Origins brand began to lose its unique identity. Initially, by being sold in a department store, Origins was positioned against other elegant brands such as Chanel and Yves St. Laurent. Against these brands, its differential advantage was that it was natural and Zen-like. But over time the referent competitive set drifted, and consumers began thinking of Origins not as a high-end department store brand but rather as a line of eco-friendly aromatherapy cosmetics. Within that competitive set, Origins' differentiating features were obscured.

Figuring out the appropriate competitive set is critical to positioning. Often this can be identified through either advertising or distribution. For example, products sold in malls are compared with other products in malls, while those sold in drugstores are compared with other drugstore brands. Advertising can also create a competitive set. By advertising 7UP as the "uncola," marketers were telling consumers to compare that drink with the best-selling colas. That set up flavor as the differentiator. Comparing 7UP instead to other lemon-flavored alternatives would have established carbonation and packaging as the differentiating factors.

To see how these three components work together, consider a product no longer on the market: Crest chewing gum. If we were to compare it with other types of gum, then the differential advantage would be its cavity-fighting potential. If, on the other hand, we were to compare it with other toothpastes, the differential advantage would be toothpaste capability in chewing gum form. A brand's differentiation depends upon both the frame of reference and the resulting strategic advantage relative to that set. The potential strengths of the product and the various comparison sets are levers that a marketer can use to find the best strategic combination. But no differential advantage will succeed if there isn't a target segment of users who value this advantage. It turns out that in the case of Crest gum, neither of the highlighted advantages was particularly appealing to consumers.

Targeting the appropriate strategic segment

The worst thing a brand can do is try and position itself for a target segment that does not exist; a brand's differential advantage must cater to a genuine customer need or want. The second worst thing a brand can do, if there is competition in the market, is to suggest that its brand is for everyone. By definition, that is mediocrity—not the best at anything, just okay at everything. With a bland positioning like that, competitive brands can cater to target segments and, with just small tweaks, better meet their needs. Catering to a unique target segment also ensures that the brand has a discernible identity.

Even when everyone ends up loving your brand, strong brands are still defined by their target segment. Think Apple: Probably almost everyone you know owns at least one Apple product, yet the Apple brand does not target everyone but rather positions itself exclusively as the brand for creative, innovative, design-minded users. Other strong brands similarly target distinct segments: Disney (children), Chanel (rich, thin fashionistas), Marlboro (rugged cowboys)—even if Every Man (or Woman) might enjoy any one of these products.

With its focus on natural skin care in an upscale market, Origins originally did that—focused on a critical segment: those who know the importance of good skin care products and could be influencers for the category. Over subsequent years, circumstances, imitation, and even the howling success of Oprah Winfrey's endorsement eroded that position. To get back on top, Origins went back to its roots.

First, it moved away from the aromatherapy associations that Oprah's strong endorsement engendered and focused once again on its skin care lines. Although the brand still offers cosmetics and bath and beauty items, the bulk of the Origins line involves skin care–related products.

Origins has also worked hard to reestablish its positioning as a proven high-performance product, while also reemphasizing its Zen and eco roots. Origins products are "powered by nature and proven by science." As the website says, the brand's two-tree logo represents its duality: "a respect for the past blended with a vision for the future, the need for inner health and outer beauty, and a respect for eastern and western cultures." Compared with other department store elite brands (the desirable reference set for Origins), this is a unique advantage. For example, MAC Cosmetics, also from the Estée Lauder Companies, features vivid color; L'Oréal Paris, a premium drugstore brand priced at department store prices, stresses luxury and glamour ("L'Oréal, because you're worth it"); while Chanel offers "perfection."

Just as important, today's Origins brand is more tightly focused on a key target segment in the United States, the 35- to 45-year-old woman who is concerned with health and with the products she chooses to put on her face. (The woman is similar in Asia, although she is younger, 25–30.) This is a knowledgeable woman who understands the importance of skin care products and chooses the best in terms of efficacy and natural ingredients. As with Apple and other category busters, the fact that Origins caters to this target segment does not limit who uses its products, but rather it builds credibility so that others decide to use the brand.

Positioning Requires Making Choices

As the Origins learning curve suggests, choosing a positioning strategy entails deciding not only what a brand is but also what it is not. Coca-Cola, for example, is "the real thing." It is tradition, family, Christmas (not by coincidence—the red we associate with Santa Claus emerged from Coke advertising). What Coke is not is a drink for the "next generation." It's neither new (recall that New Coke was a disaster) nor trendy, which leaves a gap available for another brand to position itself. And, of course, this is a gap that Pepsi is happy to fill. Pepsi is the "choice for a new generation."

The ultimate positioning of a brand should reflect the overall strategic vision of the firm. This means going beyond just product benefits. Given the costs of building a strong global awareness, a compelling brand has to be relevant today and in the future, and one that the firm can grow with. Environmental and competitive factors should help shape the positioning of the brand, but once the positioning is chosen, that focus should be consistent and serve as a blueprint for product development.

For some product-focused companies where development strategy centers solely on R&D, this is a revolutionary idea. Rather than coming up with new products using technological advances, this suggests new product development should be prioritized based on how it fits into the strategic positioning of the brand. This is a particularly difficult issue for high-technology firms that are well known for putting out state-of-the-art products that consumers do not want. Electronics firms have famously developed television recording equipment that was too complicated for anyone to use. Only when the simplified DVRs emerged did staged television viewing really take off.

Being guided by strategic brand positioning, rather than by R&D, also suggests that there may be some products that should not be produced because they will not be a good fit for the brand strategy. The first e-tablet was produced by Microsoft, but it was not a success in the market. Apple succeeded where Microsoft failed in large part because its iPad meshed perfectly with Steve Jobs's well-defined brand aesthetic and understanding of what consumers wanted—even before they themselves figured out what they wanted! Many years later, Microsoft is trying again to introduce a tablet, this time in a more mature market that's already been well defined by Apple's products. In this market, Microsoft's positioning on productivity may be a better fit for the brand.

Positioning Requires Choosing a Relevant and Desirable Advantage

While devising a positioning statement, it's important to select an advantage that is relevant and important to your target segment. Furthermore, you must be able to consistently deliver that benefit now and in the future. You also want to choose an advantage that is difficult for a competitor to copy. While your positioning is global, you must be able to deliver the advantage to your customers through your marketing mix: product features, consistent advertising and promotion, relevant channel strategy, and a consistent pricing strategy. These marketing mix tactics need to reflect the local markets.

Once a brand positioning is chosen, the core values should be communicable in a few words. A brand mantra, or brand essence, is a short (three- to five-word) phrase that captures the heart and soul of the brand and its values. A brand mantra (a) describes the ultimate benefit of the product or service offering, (b) has a descriptor that further distinguishes the function, and (c) contains an emotional component that helps delineate the benefits. Mary Kay's brand mantra can be summarized as "Enriching women's lives." That of McDonald's can be seen as "Fun family food."

21st-Century Global Brand Positioning Is Experiential

All that we have just discussed is necessary to establish brand positioning, but as we've seen, in the 21st century, marketers do not own their brands. Rather, brands are ultimately defined through the eyes of customers. As we consume brands, we begin to think of them in human terms, and form personal relationships with them. Similarly, brands over time acquire personalities of their own. Thus, even as marketers are working to differentiate their brands, they also must manage the experiential relationship customers have with the products themselves.

Brand personalities

Stanford marketing professor Jennifer Aaker has found that brand personalities can be described by using a few basic culturally established traits. For example, in America, the brand personality traits are sincerity (Coca-Cola, Timex, Hallmark), excitement (Virgin, Apple, MTV), competence (GE, IBM, CNN), sophistication (Mercedes-Benz, Tiffany, Chanel), and ruggedness (Marlboro, Levi's, Nike). In Japan, ruggedness is substituted with peacefulness. In Spain, in addition to the peacefulness substitution, passion replaces competence. In China, joyfulness replaces ruggedness, traditionalism replaces sincerity, and a new basic trait emerges: trendiness.

Brand personalities, just like human personalities, set up expectations through which the product experiences are viewed. Just as when you have a friend who is always late, you are delighted when she comes early, so brands are judged by the expectations they establish. JCrew has to define the next trend every time, or sales decline. Tiffany's must deliver elegance and sophistication, or customers are disappointed. If Coca-Cola tries extreme humor in an ad, consumers revolt. (Think of the uproar when Coke ran its famous grandma ad in which an old woman in a wheelchair starts hitting people with her cane when she can't get a Coke.) Quirky start-ups can have glitches or inventory stock-outs, but Macy's cannot.

When customers relate to brands in these kinds of human terms, they form longitudinal emotional relationships. That means marketers have to monitor the entire brand experience, from the purchase decision to how the product is used, consumed, and even discarded. The experience is tied to a social and cultural context. The brand is viewed not only rationally, but also emotionally and through the senses.

This brand experience is further shaped by interactions with the salespeople and retailers distributing and promoting the brand, with the social media communities talking and blogging about the brand, and with friends and neighbors. Probably the best example of a brand experience is Starbucks. From its home-away-from home coffee shops to its smiling baristas, Starbucks has created a world-class branded experience that differentiates its coffee products. Starbucks is also ahead of the curve in creating a social media experience—it has more than 800,000 Twitter followers and more than 5 million fans on Facebook—and in being attentive to its online audience, interacting with customers engaging on Twitter and retweeting what people say about its brand. The company also uploads videos, blog posts, and photos to its Facebook page, and it invites customers to events and hosts discussion groups. Starbucks even has a YouTube channel, and on a web page called "My Starbucks Idea" people can share any ideas related to the company and its products. People can see what others say and vote on new concepts. Employees are also encouraged to write blogs.

All brands offer customers some type of experience, but not all these experiences are good. A brand experience that is continuously managed and creatively developed to meaningfully interact with the customer adds enormous value to the overall brand positioning.

Figure 2.1
Jennifer Aaker's Dimensions of Brand Personality

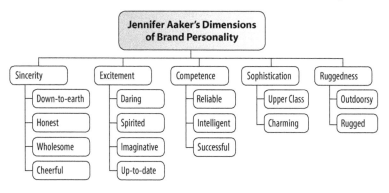

Source: Jennifer L. Aaker, "Dimensions of Brand Personality," *Journal of Marketing Research*; 34, no. 3 (Aug. 1997); ABI/INFORM Global, p. 347.

Multisensory, emotional, and social positioning

For marketers, staging this experiential positioning requires considering the emotional, behavioral, and social responses of the user. Why? Because the brand experience is interactive and co-created with the consumer. Ultimately, the brand is defined through not just the marketer's messaging, advertising, or social media strategy, but also customers' everyday experiences with the brand.

Thus, the brand must not only deliver brand benefits, but also minimize pain points. Marketers need to observe customers' experiences with the brand and note any negative perceptions, even if a bad experience results from a customer's misuse of the product. Experiential brand positioning takes the customer on a journey, every part of which needs to be managed. Multiple experiences and multiple memories form these brand relationships.

Today's modern brands are also corporate citizens, so they have to deliver more than a product experience—they have cultural and societal responsibilities as well. Brands such as Nike and Walmart are hurt if they are associated with unethical labor practices or trade relations. Brands are now expected to make the world a better place.

Bottom line, strong 21st-century brands must see far beyond the functional benefits of a product or service. They have to be managed along every consumer touch point. A brand has to be viewed within the consumption occasion, the cultural environment, and the social community. The brand positioning must resonate with consumers emotionally, appeal to their senses, make sense intellectually, and be relevant to their lifestyle—a tall challenge but a necessary one in a globally competitive environment.

An experiential branding strategy requires a full-time commitment to a multisensory, emotional, and socially responsible relationship between the customer and the brand. Developing this kind of holistic experience will build solid brands and establish a strong and sustainable competitive advantage.

Going Deep with Origins

We saw earlier how the Origins brand managed to successfully reassert itself as a uniquely differentiated brand after the "success" of Oprah's endorsement. That was how the brand got back on the battlefield, on its own terms. But how has it done with this deeper issue of experiential positioning? In essence, the brand has been an ongoing experiment in how to connect with consumers at every stage of the purchase process.

Today, the customer experience with the Origins brand most commonly begins with a discovery stage in the retail stores. Because Origins understood that customers wanted to interact with its products, it was the first department store cosmetic brand to take its products from behind the counter and put them on the wall, where a customer is able to touch them directly. The products are also organized by problem area, rather than by type of product. So instead of putting all the serums in one place, the wall is sectioned by customer-defined skin problems, such as aging, rehydration and repair, and sensitivity.

Shelf organization differs by country: The United States prefers bestsellers, whereas Asia prefers regimens. The shelf displays are augmented by customer-interaction displays that feature iPads and informational brochures. To visibly communicate the natural ingredients used in the products, the original form of the ingredients—e.g., pieces of vanilla or coffee beans—are shown on the shelves, alongside scientific beakers and instruments. To delineate the personality of the brand, Origin products have clever, light-hearted names such as A Perfect World, Checks and Balances, or Starting Over. Every visual within the store communicates the balance of nature with science, the balance of the yin and yang.

Sales associates, or "guides," as they are called, are taught not to sell but to connect with the customers and learn about their problems. The heart of the relationship with the brand is experienced through a complimentary mini-facial during which the customer can learn firsthand about the products that suit her. This interaction not only establishes relationships with the brand—between the guide and the customer—but also helps ensure appropriate use of the product and set realistic expectations.

Virtual communities augment the physical relationship. Origins has a Facebook page with nearly a half-million friends and has nearly 20,000 Twitter followers at the time of publication. These communities celebrate new products, announce concerts and other events, and provide a forum where people can discuss product experiences. Customers can also use these social media pages to request the return of discontinued product lines, to ask for help with their beauty or skin care problems, and to discover which of their own friends are using the products.

Of course, the virtual community needs to be monitored. Customers can post raves and accolades for a product, but they can just as easily post discontent. For example, a recent exchange on the Origins website notes a customer's frustration with a specific promotion not being readily available in her home store. Another customer questions Origins' commitment to animal-free testing of cosmetics. The bad news is that some of these negative comments are posted; the good news is that Origins can respond immediately and correct misconceptions. Even better, some customers stand up and refute the negative accusations, providing strong support for the Origins brand and policies.

Finally, the Origins brand has made a commitment to meet customers' needs over time but also to protect the earth they live on. Origins products are manufactured using renewable resources, wind energy, and earth-friendly practices. Because many cities do not recycle cosmetic products, Origins encourages customers to bring their used-up cosmetic tubes, bottles, and other containers (regardless of brand) to the nearest retail store to be recycled. The brand also sponsors concerts during Origins Rocks Earth Month, and Origins plants trees around the world. These activities provide the opportunity for ongoing connections with its customers.

Needless to say, all this represents an enormous investment in time and intellectual resources. Brand management is *that* hard and *that* important, and inevitably it is sometimes very intuitive for all the brand "science" that seems to underlie it. That being said, brand management can also be defended, managed, and justified through careful marketing research and measurement, both qualitatively and quantitatively. We move there next.

Chapter 3

Qualitative Measurement of Brand Value

In this chapter:

- Zaltman Metaphor Elicitation Technique
- Laddering
- Implicit Association Test
- Ethnography
- Messy Data, Valuable Insights

What a brand really represents is what consumers think it represents. Well-intentioned brand managers can take actions they think are strategically appropriate, but if these messages are not believed or accepted by the consumers, they can severely maim the brand. Netflix learned this the hard way. It might have made good business sense because of anticipated future industry changes to start charging higher prices for video streaming and separating out its video rentals into another business called Qwikster, but these actions violated consumers' core understanding of the Netflix promise. Consumers saw Netflix as the place to go to get movies conveniently. Netflix was not a particular delivery system (DVDs or streaming), and it certainly was not about dealing with two different accounts. By misunderstanding consumers' strong emotional reactions to the changes, CEO Reed Hastings undercut the brand value of Netflix catastrophically.

That's why qualitative marketing research techniques are so important. They identify the meanings consumers actually ascribe to brands, not the ones managers hope consumers will take away. But getting the right read takes hard work.

The Netflix decision was egregious. It's quite possible that if Netflix had simply asked its consumers directly, they would have openly complained about the change. But we can only guess this in hindsight. Conventional marketing research surveys may not have identified this extreme reaction. Why? Perhaps surprisingly, in marketing surveys, consumers tend to be remarkably pliable. When asked, they feed back what they think they are supposed to say, rather than what they are truly thinking. Especially, when as often happens, the question is framed from the management perspective. Since consumers don't spend much time consciously dwelling on brands, the wording of the question frames how managers think consumers should think about the brand. The art of good marketing research is to find creative ways to probe consumers' minds and uncover what they are actually thinking, feeling, and responding to automatically, without having the mere process of asking the questions influence the answers.

Several methodologies exist to uncover these deep meanings, each based on a different theoretical framework and set of assumptions. One class of techniques uses psychological probing, almost like psychoanalysis, to uncover deep-seated emotions and thoughts. The best-known method in this class is the Zaltman metaphor elicitation technique (ZMET), developed by Gerald Zaltman, a Harvard emeritus professor. ZMET is based on the premise that people use visual metaphors to express their unspoken ideas about brands. The researcher's job, then, is to uncover those metaphors.

Another, similar technique is called laddering. The basic question in the laddering technique is why? Consumers are asked why they use a particular brand, and then why that reason makes sense, and so on. Eventually, these answers are used to "ladder up" to deep underlying motivations and life values.

The implicit association test, as the name suggests, measures implicit associations or attitudes. Consumers are thought to have explicit attitudes that they can express when asked, and implicit attitudes that they cannot consciously control. The harder-to-access, implicit attitudes can form visceral responses to brands that may help marketers predict behavior.

Finally, ethnographic methodologies are used to understand the way culture affects behavior. The priority in ethnographic research is to make sure the data collection occurs in natural settings and is based primarily on observation. The assumption here is that true behavior can be observed only in its own cultural contexts and that traditional marketing research techniques using surveys or experiments take place outside of the natural environment and thus have an artificial component.

Zaltman Metaphor Elicitation Technique

The Zaltman Metaphor Elicitation Technique (ZMET) is designed to probe the deep recesses of consumers' minds. The premise is that when consumers think about brands, they do so in images and metaphors, not in words. Much of the communication between people is nonverbal. During a conversation, if a person says one thing about a brand but implies something else through body language, most often people will trust the body language. The same, ZMET holds, is true of brands. People may say one thing but associate different, nonverbal imagery with the brand, and in the end the imagery is more central to their understanding of the brand.

The ZMET is designed to identify and elicit the metaphors that consumers use to tell stories about brands. The assumption underlying the process is that there are three layers of metaphor. The first level, surface metaphors, is used in everyday language. ZMET refers to these surface connections as the tip of the iceberg. An example of this can be seen through Budweiser advertising. One very famous ad for Budweiser shows different people speaking on the telephone and inquiring, "Wassup?" The surface metaphor is that these people are connected by a telephone conversation.

The second level of metaphor runs just below the surface and is not completely buried in the unconscious. In this ad, the second-level metaphor is that drinking beer together also connects these people.

The third level is deep metaphor. This is really the heart of the ZMET. Many international marketing gurus will talk about differences among cultures, but as noted in the introduction, true global brands have universal meaning. That concept is similar in ZMET. The key to ZMET is that relatively few universal values or metaphors hold for human beings across cultures and geographies, and that these are the really influential and powerful ones. (The ZMET, it should be noted, shares many intellectual roots with the theory of literary archetypes and Carl Jung's collective unconscious.)

In the Budweiser example just given, the deep metaphor is a universal one: the concept of connection, which refers to the deep need people have to feel like they belong somewhere, the deep understanding of what it feels like to be kept in the loop. So the surface metaphor is connection just by speaking on the phone and all asking, "Wassup?" The metaphor just under the surface is connection through social engagement and drinking beer together, and the deep metaphor is the deep-seated need to feel connected, to feel that sense of belonging. Budweiser consistently uses this connection metaphor throughout its advertising, whether the subjects are frogs, donkeys, people, or even Bud's famous Clydesdale horses. When this association is made consistently over time, a neural network develops in the consumers' minds. When this happens it is difficult for other brands in the category to use the same association as effectively.

Universal deep metaphors

ZMET recognizes seven metaphors as the most universal and powerful: balance, transformation, journey, container, resource, control, and the connection metaphor already noted. Using ZMET, surface metaphors are collected from consumers about specific brands. Then skilled interviewers link these tip-of-the-iceberg metaphors to one or more of the deeper metaphors. Once a universal metaphor is identified, this becomes the conduit through which to communicate messaging about the brand.

An example: A premium vodka brand was linked to the deep metaphor of balance, which includes ideas of equilibrium and can refer to moral balance, social balance, or aesthetic balance. Once this metaphor was identified, the advertising and brand symbolism for the vodka circulated around this idea. The vodka was shown to be a balance between the natural elements represented by the freshness of the ingredients on the one hand and the nature of the distilling process that changed these ingredients into alcohol on the other. The brand slogans focused on the importance of the right ingredients in the right hands to produce an alcohol with class. Advertising for the vodka showed glasses that were balanced upon one another in a pyramid structure of three. The imagery spoke to the balance without using words.

The deep metaphor identified for Michelin tires was container. Containers keep things in and keep things out. They can protect or trap us, and can be positive or negative. Memory is a container because it stores individual histories. Human beings themselves are containers of blood, bones, and so on. Culture is a container of specific norms. For Michelin, the tire was visualized as a superficial metaphor, a container, which stood for the deeper metaphor of container as safety. To illustrate the superficial level, one advertisement showed a baby seated inside a tire with pairs of stuffed animals. The tire here was a metaphor for Noah's ark. The well-known ad slogan, "Michelin, because so much is riding on your tires" alludes to the deeper metaphor of container as safety. Without using the actual word "safety" anywhere, the idea is still powerfully communicated.

ZMET interview

Once a company engages ZMET experts to identify the underlying metaphors for its brand, at least 20 consumers familiar with the brand are recruited. The individuals are asked to collect a minimum of 12 images that represent their thoughts and feelings about the brand. They can use the Internet, snap photos, or search through magazines, but they are cautioned not to think too deeply about this—just collect photographs that seem to them to portray the brand. Each participant typically spends about five hours collecting these images.

A ZMET researcher then interviews the participants. In each interview is very involved, the respondent is asked to describe each image and tell a story about it. Participants are then asked to sort the images into meaningful groups and to provide a label for each group. Laddering techniques (described later) are also used. Next come myriad questions about the most representative image, any missing images, and which other image not selected might be opposite of the brand. Participants are also asked to think about the sensory aspects of the brand: colors, sounds, and emotions. The interviewer then typically gets the respondent to create a mental map for the brand and a summary collage of the images, with a concluding vignette. Much like a typical session with a therapist, these interviews are designed to uncover the deep metaphors that reside beneath the surface of the chosen imagery.

The goal of the process is to develop the strategic metaphor or set of metaphors for the brand that will capture the core meaning of the marketing strategy. One example of some insights that came out of the ZMET process is the branding strategy for Motorola. The ZMET process found that the Motorola brand was associated with imagery of dogs. Probing into this, researchers found that the canines represented comfort and security. Motorola was seen as a loyal animal that was taking care of them. The implication from the research was that the Motorola product should not be seen as technology but more as a watchdog.

Laddering

Laddering is designed to get at the deep underlying motivations in consumers for purchasing a product so that a differentiating positioning strategy for a brand can be created. And since this positioning will be built on understanding why consumers buy in the category, it should be a positioning strategy that will resonate.

The process starts with a few focus groups to identify key product attributes and features that define the product. Since the subsequent individual laddering interviews will need to be aggregated, it is important to start with a standardized set of attributes that represents the critical criteria for the majority of the target segment.

Once the key attributes are identified, interviewees are asked to provide two benefits associated with each attribute. For example, a feature of a hair product might be "holds hair in place." The respondent would be asked what benefit that provided. Perhaps he'd say that it would decrease the time he spent fussing with his hair and lend more time to doing other things. After the benefit is provided, the interviewer "ladders up" by asking why that benefit is important. Perhaps the respondent will say he needs to get a lot of things done. He is again asked why, and the interview continues to ladder up until a terminal value is achieved. For example, in this illustration, one might ladder up until the participant says, "Because I want to accomplish something with my life." Or perhaps the process will ladder up to, "Because getting things done makes me feel better about myself, and my self-esteem is improved."

This process is repeated for each attribute or feature, and is done for a reasonable-sized sample of target users for the product. A hierarchical values map is then created for each respondent. This is basically a summary mapping that shows how the features ladder up to terminal values. Several attributes may reach the same terminal values, perhaps through different paths. Generally, these maps result in three or four terminal values, even though they start with eight or nine product features.

To aggregate these maps over several individuals, one needs first to standardize the language across the respondents. So similar concepts and ideas are labeled with the same words, even if subtle differences exist from individual to individual. Then an aggregate map is created by including the relationships mentioned by the majority of respondents. Stronger relationships are usually indicated by a thicker connecting line. Clearly, there is some art to this aggregation process, but similar ideas are frequently repeated across respondents, and those are the ones included. A skilled interviewer is required to uncover some of the more subtle relationships that consumers may not readily admit to. For example, consumers may not admit right away that they buy Coach handbags for the prestige it affords them. Experience is also generally needed to produce a reasonable aggregate map.

When these maps are correctly produced, they illustrate the means, or attributes, that the product has to produce benefits and how those means provide consequences for the consumers, which results in delivering to their personal values. As such, this approach is also sometimes called a means-consequences-ends model.

Using laddering, the terminal values associated with a product can differ across cultures, because the relative importance of various values can change across cultures and demographics. In keeping with the theory behind ZMET, the overall set of terminal values stays constant, but the relative importance changes. For example, one study suggested that freedom as a value was very important in France, Italy, and Spain but not as important in China. Stable relationships were very important in the United Kingdom and Japan but less so in Venezuela. Ambition mattered a great deal in Egypt and Saudi Arabia but less so in Italy. Romance was more important in Thailand than in India.

These values differed in importance across age groups as well. While protecting family and honesty was a universal value across all age groups, the importance of friendship and self-esteem was much more important for younger consumers, while health and fitness and justice gained in importance for older people.

Understanding the relationship between the product-class attributes and the relative importance of different values can help a brand decide on the best positioning strategy. Juicy Fruit gum engaged in a laddering market research study to understand why young people liked the gum. Prior to the research, brand managers hypothesized that consumers might like the gum because it relieved stress or could compensate for lack of opportunity to brush their teeth. The research, though, showed that the chief reason for liking the gum was that it was sweet and energizing, which made consumers more productive and increased their sense of achievement. In subsequent advertising, the slogan "Gotta have sweet?" was used to capitalize on this new knowledge.

Implicit Association Test

The Implicit Association Test (IAT) measures unconscious or automatic associations that are so well learned that operate outside of conscious awareness. The process was originally designed to measure stereotypes and attitudes that people knew were socially undesirable but unwittingly continued to have anyway.

Measuring the IAT response is complicated, but the idea behind it is fairly intuitive. Automatic associations are fast, while those you have to think about take just a little longer to connect. That difference in timing is measured as the IAT effect. The process almost always requires several trials. The IAT is usually administered on a computer. Respondents are asked to hit a key on the left side of the keyboard (say, "d") to indicate that they are observing one kind of stimuli, and on the right, (say, "k") if another kind of stimuli is named. But those are just the mechanics of the test; the speed of making an association is what is measured.

As an example, consider running an IAT on the four suits in a deck of cards. The easy associations will be between the red suits (hearts and diamonds) and the black suits (spades and clubs). The IAT methodology would then require you to hit a "d" if a heart or diamond appeared on the screen or a "k" if a spade or club appeared on the screen. Associating those suits with each other can be done automatically and quickly. However, if we asked you to link a club (black) with a diamond (red) and hit "d" if either of those appeared, you could do it, but it would take more time. You would have to override your natural associations. This additional time in making the connection is considered the IAT effect. Similarly, if you associate a brand such as Tinkertoys with children, it would be quick and automatic to make that connection. If we ask you to associate Tinkertoys with senior citizens, you could do it, but it would take a little bit of time because it is not an automatic reaction. Again this increase in reaction time, even if it is very, very short, is considered the IAT effect.

For branding purposes, evaluative words can be linked with brands that are thought to be automatic associations versus those that are not automatic, and one can identify what is automatically associated with a brand by the difference in timing. Thus, one can use adjectives such as "good" or "bad,"and then two brands, say, a national brand such as Kraft and the store brand. The IAT effect would measure the time it took to hit the correct key if "Kraft" or "good" were shown versus the time it took to hit the correct key if "Kraft" or "bad" were shown, and similarly this could be done for the store brand. If consumers implicitly assumed that the national brand was better, it would take them less time to hit the appropriate key when "Kraft" was associated with "good" than when it was associated with "bad." Or one could test Apple versus Dell using adjectives such as "creative" and "routine."

My coauthors and I ran an IAT study testing the effect known as pharmaceutical detailing—i.e., when pharmaceutical companies provide doctors with branded marketing materials. Our study was run on university medical students to test their implicit attitudes toward branded (as opposed to generic) pharmaceutical products. Prior to the experiment, the medical students were asked to fill out some paperwork on either a clipboard with no branding or one stamped with the Lipitor brand. We found that the experimental manipulation had no effect on the students' explicit attitudes toward the brand and no effect on their prescribing decision making as measured by direct questioning. However, the manipulation did affect their implicit attitudes toward the Lipitor brand as measured by the IAT. On one campus, where the medical community was actively protesting the pharmaceutical industry's marketing practices, exposure to the branded clipboard lowered implicit attitudes toward the national brand. However, on another campus, where there was no protesting and where detailing was accepted, exposure to the branded clipboard increased positive associations with the Lipitor brand.

The IAT methodology is not used that often in commercial branding studies, but it provides an opportunity to measure attitudes that consumers either do not realize they hold or are reluctant to admit.

Ethnography

Ethnography is the study—traditionally by anthropologists, but in the case of branding, by market researchers—of the cultural environment of a specific group. The intent of ethnography is to provide a "thick description," or a detailed insider's understanding, of the culture that surrounds a subgroup's behaviors. A key aspect of this approach is that the researcher observes the behavior in a natural environment and lets the meanings emerge from the encounter rather than imposing any structure or framework on the observational process.

Marketing researchers have adopted this methodology for observing consumer culture in order to understand exactly how consumers use products and services. This approach focuses on the cultural and social practices surrounding the behavior rather than on the cognitive aspects. Research observers watch, learn, and listen to consumers as they engage in consumer rituals.

Consumer anthropologists will watch people in their kitchens or bathrooms to see how products fit into daily routines. (This isn't Peeping Tom–style work; respondents are paid to allow the ethnographers into their homes.) For example, anthropologic research discovered that many consumers think of the shower as a form of retreat, a place to get away from the stresses of daily life. They observed the rituals people follow using liquid soap—pumping it slowly onto a loofah or washcloth and sudsing it up before applying. (Obviously, with shower observation, swimsuits are allowed as a concession to modesty.) Similarly, researchers observe people eating to study the rituals surrounding meals. Researchers have followed respondents into dressing rooms to see how they try on clothes or have watched them at outdoor barbecues. All these observations give insights to the connections people feel with products and help inform packaging, advertising, and new-product design decisions.

A well-known example of an anthropological approach involved studying the rituals of Thanksgiving in order to understand the best ways to promote products for holiday purchase. One observation that emerged from the study is that a key component of the holiday dinner is an overabundance of dishes on the table, since each member of the party has a certain favorite that needs to be represented. This suggests, for example, that for Thanksgiving more forms of cranberry sauce are preferable to fewer, and the marketing of the sauces should feature this. Cranberry sauces at Thanksgiving are like pies for desserts—more variety is better. Happily, bounteous leftovers are also part of the Thanksgiving experience.

Features of ethnographic research

Several decisions need to be made in implementing consumer ethnographic research. One key question is whether the researcher observes as a participant or as an outsider. The advantage of being a participant in the consumption occasion is that the researcher gets access to the "backstage" areas of the behaviors. In observing consumers' behaviors at mealtimes, a guest at the table has better access to the pre- and post-meal activities and can be a part of the conversations and discussions. But being a participant does change what actually occurs and can bias perspective in interpretation.

If the researcher chooses nonparticipation, then the behavior occurs more naturally. Nonparticipant observation can be done through personal observation or, more commonly, through video recording. Many retail environments have video recorders, primarily installed for security reasons but now also for tracking retail patterns within a store. The video cameras can observe the paths consumers use within the store, how long they stand in front of a particular category, whether they consult others in the purchase process, whether they touch a product, and so on. Video cameras have recorded behavior in parking lots (used to inform decision making for Park & Ride programs), in infant changing rooms (used to inform decisions for a diaper company), in children's playrooms (used to inform decisions for a toy company), and at many other locations. Some retailers are now tracking the location of people's smartphones within a store to monitor their shopping patterns.

The data collected can then be enhanced by conducting ethnographic interviews—encouraging respondents to provide value-laden stories, their own selective memories, and freely expressed emotions, judgments, and experiences. Unlike other types of research that seeks to obtain an unbiased record, here the data collected must be credible to the participant.

Aggregation and organization of these data into a coherent account take professional attention. Ethnographic researchers look to develop a detailed account that represents the many layers involved. They look for redundancy and variety, and search for credible representations of the events.

Messy Data, Valuable Insights

These different qualitative research techniques are all designed to help firms understand what is going on in the minds of consumers. They provide consumer insight and so may call into question fundamental assumptions a firm is making.

Since these techniques probe deeply into consumers' minds, the data are of necessity messy and idiosyncratic. As such, they are unstructured and difficult to aggregate. Further, sampling bias is a huge problem in interpretation. Even with the help of video cameras that allow for the collection of behavior across a large sample, creating a cohesive summary of behavior is challenging. Without mechanical help, personal interviewing methods are expensive and limit the ultimate size of the sample. Personal interviews are also subject to interview bias.

On the plus side, these methods are critical for understanding consumers' lives; seeing how products and services fit into behaviors, relationships, and goals; and ultimately understanding the relationship consumers have with brands. But given the limitations of small sample sizes, biased interpretation, and problems in generalization, many different methodologies should be used to triangulate the findings and look for convergent results.

Good qualitative research, interpreted correctly, can then be used to generate the hypotheses, frameworks, and structures to be tested on large sample sizes and analyzed using conventional quantitative methods. We will explore these quantitative methods, and methods that assess how to prove a monetary valuation for the brand asset or brand equity, in the next chapter.

Chapter 4

Quantitative Methods for Assessing Brand Value

In this chapter:

• Customer-Based Evaluations of Brand Effectiveness
• Brand Valuation Measurement
• Market Value/Shareholder Value
• Using Quantitative Measurement to Guide Action

Building brands is hard work and very expensive. The payoff, of course, is that a great brand is a tremendous asset. Interbrand estimates that the *50th*-place finisher in its 2012 ranking of top US retail brands, Rent-A-Center, is worth $771 million. The top retailer brand of them all, Walmart, gets valued at a staggering $139 billion. (Interbrand's methodology will be discussed later.)

Building the brand correctly is not a given. Just as some brands prove to be gold mines, others end up as sinkholes that can swallow corporate resources. As with any marketing activity, the surest way to assess whether a brand is meeting its goals and fulfilling its strategic objectives is through quantitative measurement, which can then provide benchmarks for performance and evaluation.

One set of measures reflects how customers evaluate your brand. You need to measure reactions at every stage of the customer decision-making process. Is your brand in a customer's evoked set? Is it emotionally valued and one that customers are highly willing to recommend? Answers to these critical questions demand reliable and valid metrics. Another set of measures quantifies brand equity. Being able to put a value on brand equity helps justify the resources allocated to building a brand.

Customer-Based Evaluations of Brand Effectiveness

Marketing research surveys via mall intercepts, telephone interviews, mail, and (more and more frequently) the Internet can assess the attitudes and beliefs of brand customers', and those of competitors' customers.

Brand attitudes and perceptions can be measured both historically and prospectively, and in real time at various actual and digital customer touch points. Measuring attitudes in real time allows a company to respond immediately to consumer comments and to open up a consumer dialogue. This can be especially valuable if done online and in a social community.

Brand awareness

Brand awareness—the accessibility of the brand in memory—can occur accidentally, through word of mouth, or at the time of purchase. Most brand marketing activity, such as television advertising, online advertising, public relations activity, and celebrity endorsement, is directed to this end, but brand awareness is multitiered. Brand managers should be concerned with both the *depth* of awareness (i.e., how many consumers know the brand, how well they know it) and the *breadth* of awareness (such as under which circumstances the brand comes to mind. With mature brands, this latter area is frequently a problem. Whereas mature brands are likely to be known by many, they may not be recalled easily under certain circumstances. For example, while Dunkin' Donuts is a well-known brand, it might come to mind only when consumers think about breakfast and not be easily recalled at dinnertime, even though doughnuts could seemingly be a fine dinner dessert.

Brand awareness comes in three levels. The first, the gold standard, is unaided recall, where high top-of-mind awareness is the goal. Unaided recall is measured by asking consumers to name brands without giving them any cues. The easier the brand name comes to mind, and the more often it does under various circumstances, the higher the top-of-mind awareness for that brand. For example, if consumers were asked to name a cola, Coca-Cola would likely be either the first or second brand named. If consumers were asked to name a soft drink, Coke would rank high. If they were asked to name a beverage, Coke would likely remain on top. Coke would remain on top for some people even if they were asked to name a food or an American brand. That's extraordinary brand awareness. Everyone knows the brand, and everyone can find the brand in memory in a variety of contexts.

To get a more nuanced measure of unaided recall, a researcher can record the order that brands come to mind along with how long it takes for this to happen. The first brands mentioned have the highest top-of-mind awareness. In addition, the pattern of recall can give insight into how the brand knowledge is organized in memory. Brands tend to be recorded in categorical clusters. Brands that are grouped together are likely to share associations. The clusters may also hint at consumers' consideration sets.

The next level of brand awareness is aided recall. Here, cues are used, but the brand name itself is withheld. Sometimes occasions are used as an aid: What brand of candy would you buy at the movies? Others help bring back the advertising and symbols that cue the brand: What's the name of the blimp that hovers over a sports stadium? What brand do you think of when you see a red swoosh? In thinking about paper towels, can you name the "quicker picker-upper"? Or, with fashion brands, you might probe attributes: Can you name the brand that has the beige-black-and-red plaid fabric?

The lowest level of awareness is simple brand recognition. Questions such as "Do you recognize the brand A&W?" or "Have you seen the brand Parker recently?" help customers recall brands that would not come to mind unaided. This is still very valuable awareness, as research shows that familiar brands are preferred. You might have experienced this phenomenon yourself—perhaps when you were drawn to brands from home that you recognized while in a foreign supermarket, especially brands you would not normally have purchased. True recognition (as opposed to false memories or the tendency of respondents to try to please the researcher) can be determined by including decoys or brands that do not exist—Tide dishwashing liquid, for example.

Brand attitudes

Awareness counts, obviously, but it's also important to know whether consumers have positive associations and attitudes with a brand per se and vis-à-vis competing brands. To do this, marketers measure brand attitudes. In chapter 3, we discussed how to surreptitiously uncover associations from consumers. These data are more difficult to quantify. Marketers seeking more quantitative measures are apt to rely on closed-ended questions that probe the strength, favorability, and uniqueness of various attributes or benefits associated with the brand.

For example, you might ask. To what extent do you agree that the following characteristics are descriptive of the BMW brand? (agree/disagree on a 7-point scale)
- High performance
- Good value
- Style

Then you can ask about the importance of these variables (on an important/unimportant 7-point scale), and a weighted average model can be used to assess the overall attitude toward the brand. If performance was weighted as a 7 and BMW had a score of 7 on this attribute, if value was weighted as a 5 and BMW had a score of 6 on this attribute, and if style was weighted as a 6 and BMW had a score of 3 on that attribute, then BMW's overall attitude measure would be $7*7 + 5*6 + 6*3 = 97$.

You also can determine how BMW compares with other brands by either assessing the uniqueness of BMW on the various dimensions or measuring how other brands perform on these attributes. This technique can equally be used to measure emotional dimensions, and functional benefits associated with the brand.

The advantage of this approach is that you have an overall score for each brand and can monitor that score over time. In addition, you can determine prescriptive actions to improve brand attitudes. Should BMW score high on an unimportant attribute, marketers can set out to convince consumers of the merits of that attribute through various strategies. If BMW scores low on an important attribute, the company can work either to fix the perception that underlies the low score or to improve the performance on that attribute if that is the problem.

The disadvantage of this approach is that the attributes are predetermined and usually follow conventional thinking. In other words, if I am assessing attitudes toward the brand Revlon, I might measure attitudes about color, ease of use, and price. If those are the attributes that consumers use to assess cosmetics, this will give me a good idea about brand attitudes. But if consumers think about cosmetic brands based on other attributes—for example, whether they do animal testing or whether the brand is hypoallergenic—then the brand attitude measurement will be invalid.

Thus, one negative aspect of this traditional approach to measuring attitude is that important attributes may be omitted from the analysis, while unimportant attributes are included and thus overweighted. Further, there is an implicit assumption that the attributes that are included are positive. For example, MAC Cosmetics might score high on exotic colors, but for some consumers this may be a negative feature.

Brand loyalty

Assessing brand loyalty is largely a matter of measuring satisfaction, and perhaps the best predictor of that is whether customers are likely to purchase the same brand again. Traditional measures of satisfaction include responses such as (agree/disagree on a 7- point scale):

- I am fully satisfied with Starbucks.
- If a Starbucks shop were not nearby, I would travel to find one.
- I plan to visit a Starbucks shop within the week.
- I would recommend Starbucks to a friend.

Through the use of loyalty cards and website tracking, behavioral measures can be added to the arsenal of feedback mechanisms. These measures determine brand loyalty based not only on what people say, but also on what they do—that is, how they actually behave. We can measure trial, repeat, frequency of visit, recency (how recently the customer used the product), and depth of behavior (quantity purchased, time spent on the site, and so on). These measures can help illuminate the engagement level of customers toward specific brands. Measuring shopping behavior online, including shopping cart abandonment or subscription cancellation, also allows marketers to see exactly where in the decision process customers drop out. For example, if a consumer was visiting the Neiman Marcus website, her viewing behavior could be parsed to show how many pages into the website she visited, how long she spent on each page, whether she put items in a shopping cart, and whether she proceeded to check out.

Brand ambassadors—brand referral

Customers have now become co-creators of brand identity; they blog, tag, like, pin, and tweet about products. This consumer-generated content not only reflects the users' opinions about brands, but also serves as a second-order sounding board for evaluating the marketing of the brand. Many companies are using Facebook campaigns to determine whether abandoned products should be brought back. For example, Bobbi Brown and MAC, both Estée Lauder companies, ran Facebook campaigns so that fans could vote on whether to bring back certain discontinued makeup colors. Companies are also using their Facebook pages to run focus groups. Frito-Lay recently asked fans to vote on new flavors for chips by clicking on an "I'd Eat That" button. Gilt Groupe has set up Facebook chats to learn about what products customers are interested in.

Consumer online reviews, blogs, and evaluations can be seen as credible and trustworthy sources for other consumers. In addition to monitoring the content of this messaging, companies can and should weigh the actual influence of the most active brand ambassadors. For example, Klout measures the online influence of customers who communicate about a brand and assigns them a Klout score. A similar service, PeerIndex, now operates in the United Kingdom. Twitalyzer measures who are the most influential people on Twitter.

Using these measures to diagnose the problem

With these measurement techniques, managers can assess where the brand is falling short in the consumer decision-making process and strategize ways to fix the problem. If the brand has limited breadth of awareness, managers can devise strategies to make sure that consumers do not overlook the brand in uncommon circumstances. Slogans such as "Wow, I could have had a V-8," Maxwell House coffee's "It's not just for breakfast anymore," and Taco Bell's "Think outside the bun" aim to expand awareness outside conventional situations.

If attitudes about the brand image are not positive, managers know that they have to establish a more persuasive point of difference. Similarly, if there is little buzz or referral about the brand, the brand is not creating a compelling experience. These measures help marketers fine-tune their activity and provide feedback mechanisms. It is critical to monitor these measures over time (perhaps in a dashboard) to establish trends. Changes in measures, even subtle ones, can help catch a problem before it becomes uncorrectable.

Brand Valuation Measurement

Since brand building is an expensive investment, profit-oriented firms need to have some measure of the brand as an asset to justify the expenditure. Brand value measures—unlike the measures just described, which address the awareness, positioning, and image—attempt to assign an actual dollar value to the brand that can then be used on the balance sheet to represent the brand asset. In addition, monitoring brand value over time using leading and lagging measures can alert managers to potential problems if a brand starts to lose value. It also helps justify resource allocation strategies. Arguing that resources should be devoted to marketing and brand-building activities is an uphill fight absent any quantification of the value of the brand.

How you assess brand value is another matter. One technique measures the costs that have been incurred in building the brand. A second attempts to measure the income of price premium that the brand adds to the bottom line over and above the cost of goods sold. Finally, there are approaches that attempt to provide a market value. The two most well-known models here are Interbrand, cited earlier, and the BrandAsset Valuator model.

Cost approaches

Cost approaches to brand value attempt to assess the expense of replacing the brand as it exists today, an often iffy calculation. First, historic expenses to build the brand—R&D, and marketing and advertising costs—may not correlate with current expenses. What's more, in an older marketplace with fewer competitors, gaining brand awareness was relatively easy. In today's cluttered marketplace, reproducing this level of brand awareness could take several times the investment. Also, marketers might have spent money in the past for inefficient advertisements and marketing activity that did little to add to the brand value. And, of course, costs in the past may not correlate at all with current or future costs. If unsuccessful brand activities can be eliminated, the cost approach might reflect the minimum required to reproduce the brand value.

One use of a cost approach is to calculate what is known as Tobin's Q, which is a measure of profitability. Tobin's Q is defined as the:

$$(\text{market value}) / (\text{replacement value})$$

The idea here is that a brand is very profitable if its worth in the marketplace is significantly higher than the costs it took or would take to reproduce it. For example, Coke has a Tobin's Q at greater than 2. Other companies with high Q ratios include Coach and Apple, while retailers with lower Tobin's Q would be convenience stores and Woolworth's.

Income approach

The income approach is more of a product-market calculation. This methodology measures how much revenue a branded good would produce over and above what that exact same product would produce if it were unbranded. There are various ways to do this. If there's an equivalent generic product, then one can compute the profits earned by a branded good over and above those earned by the generic or store-brand equivalent minus the branding costs. If there is not a comparable nonbranded equivalent, market research techniques such as conjoint or trade-off analysis can be used to compute the price premium garnered by the branded product over a nonbranded equivalent. Other pure-revenue plays, such as licensing fees, can also be computed for this approach.

The difficulty with this approach is finding the appropriate generic equivalent, but in theory, this process does measure the market value of the brand, or its profitability, in current market terms. However, it does not aggregate up over the lifetime of the brand to determine its value as an asset to the firm, and therefore this method cannot by itself be used to justify the allocation of resources within the firm. The two models we discuss next, Interbrand and the BrandAsset Valuator, were created precisely to provide these kinds of holistic brand values.

Market Value/Shareholder Value

The market value/shareholder value approach to brand valuation is one that tries to price the brand as an asset or to determine how much an open market would be willing to pay for the brand trademark itself. This is difficult to do because an open market for brands does not exist unless a company is sold. Sometimes the amount paid over and above book value is considered the premium due to the brand equity involved. The approaches generally used attempt to measure the present value of the future economic benefit of the brand. In essence, the methodology equates the brand valuation to a stock valuation. Although many models do this, and many different market research firms attempt it, probably the best known one is the Interbrand model.

Interbrand model

The Interbrand approach looks at both the income statement and the balance sheet and computes how they interact to estimate brand value. Interbrand uses an economic value added (EVA) analysis of business unit performance to calculate how much profit is added to the firm through its brand asset. The overall brand valuation is a function of both current and future earnings, and considers a risk-adjusted charge for capital to generate the branded profits. Using this kind of measure, the firm can consider the efficiency of the resources allocated to brand building. Interbrand maintains, therefore, that its methodology reflects the effect of brand activity on shareholder value and not just on cash flow.

Three critical inputs make up Interbrand's valuation process:

1. **Calculate how much profit is added to the firm from all its intangibles.** This is done by starting with the firm's revenues and deducting all costs, including opportunity costs of the tangible assets that are employed (e.g., opportunity costs of plant, property, and working capital) and taxes. What's left are the earnings due to intangible assets—usually labeled by accountants as "goodwill." In addition to the profit generated by "brand equity," this figure can also include intangibles such as patents, skill of the management, customer relations, and geographic advantages, and more brand-specific advantages such as trademark and licensing agreements.

2. **Determine the percentage of those intangible earnings that should be a function of brand equity, or the per-centage due to brand alone.** Interbrand has several methods for doing this. No matter how it is determined—by market research field studies, expert panels, or simulations or judgment models—this percentage can vary widely by industry. For example, in the perfume business, approximately 95% of intangible earnings are due to brand. With beer, it's 85%. In financial services, the estimate is 40%; in hotels, 30%. Of course, these are estimates and industry averages, and they can vary a lot by brand. Once this percentage is calculated, it is multiplied by the earnings due to the intangible assets, to determine the branded earnings. These branded earnings can be forecast for the current year as well as for the next five years. Obviously, the ones for years two through five reflect assumptions about market and market share growth, as well as cost estimates.

3. **Measure the brand strength—its relevance and how well it can execute.** This measure is used to discount the value of future earnings from the brand. Brand strength is scored on a scale of 0 to 100, and that score is used to determine the rate that will be used to discount future branded earnings to a present value. The brand strength score is a function of ratings on multiple criteria: clarity of the brand, brand commitment, brand protection aspects, consistency of the brand, support for the brand, authenticity of the brand, and so on.

The brand-strength score is then used to compute a discount rate tied to the discount rate on the 10-year US Treasury note. (Interbrand uses the 10-year Treasury note rate because historically it has been stable and has a low risk of volatility.) The math here gets complicated, but the bottom line is that high brand scores, like high bond valuations, raise value because they have lower discount rates. The discount rate is used to compute the net present value for the first five years using the branded profits that were computed in step two. Then the perpetuity value is computed: perpetuity value = (forecasted branded profits Y6) / (discount rate minus the growth rate). This is the standard way to compute the perpetuity value (or limit) for calculating the lifetime value of assets. This computed perpetuity value is added to the net present value of the branded profits for the first five years, and this is the final valuation number.

In summary, then, the Interbrand method first calculates the earnings from intangibles for the firm. From this number, it calculates the percentage of those earnings that are due to the brand. Then Interbrand calculates the level of risk associated with this forecast as a function of the brand strength. The stronger the brand, the lower the risk, and the less the earnings are discounted. Finally, a net present value is computed, assuming that the brand will exist for a long time.

Using this methodology, Interbrand has produced values for the top 100 global brands for the past few years. For example, in 2012 Interbrand valued the Coca-Cola brand as being worth $77.8 billion, Apple as $76.6 billion, IBM as $75.5 billion, Google as $68.7 billion, and Microsoft as $57.8 billion. Powerful global brands that act more like niche brands are valued much lower. The Ferrari brand is pegged at $3.6 billion by the Interbrand model, Harley-Davidson at $3.5 billion, and Starbucks at $3.7 billion. High-end luxury brands, which are clearly valuable brand names but relate to a small, elite target market, never have the same investment value as the top brands. For example, Armani is valued at $3.8 billion and Burberry at $3.7 billion. These brand valuations can also be calculated longitudinally, to measure the effects of market activity on the brand.

BrandAsset Valuator (BAV) model

Another well-known model used to calculate brand value over time is the BrandAsset Valuator, developed by the WPP Group's BAV Consulting. This model is reportedly based on the longest-running study of brands in the world. Begun in 1993, the database has been gleaned from an ongoing survey of more than 800,000 consumers in 50 countries and includes 47,000 brands. This analysis is category agnostic, provides current and leading indicators, and can be tied to financial valuations.

The core principle of this model is that brands develop in a very specific progression of consumer perceptions, which is represented by "Four Pillars of Brand Health." The first and primary pillar is Energized Differentiation, which relates to the brand's point of difference and to the margins it can generate. The second pillar is Relevance, or how appropriate the brand is to the general consumer, which is related to consideration and trial. The third, Esteem, reflects the popularity and quality of the brand and relates to loyalty. The final pillar is Knowledge, or the consumer's understanding of the brand, which relates to brand saliency and familiarity.

Each brand in the BAV database can be measured on these four pillars, and the different patterns of the pillars can help diagnose the characteristics of the specific brand in the market-place. For example, if a brand has a high value on Energized Differentiation but a lower value on Relevance, that brand has the power to build more Relevance and has room to grow. Examples of this in the database include Kindle and Zappos. However, if the brand has great Relevance but little Differentiation, then the uniqueness of the brand has faded and the brand can become a commodity, competing mostly on price or convenience. See, for example, Kleenex, Fruit of the Loom, and Shell gasoline. Brands with high Energized Differentiation and Esteem benefit from positive brand experience (Sony and Nike, for example), while brands that exhibit high Differentiation but low Esteem (such as

Spike TV, *Jersey Shore*, and Hooters) can be polarizing brands or guilty pleasures. Brands with high Esteem and low Knowledge are better liked than known (including Under Armour, Dogfish Head Ale, and Kevlar). Brands that have high Knowledge but low Esteem (such as Marlboro, Motel 6, or bp) are well known but not well liked. Understanding these different relationships among the four pillars gives diagnostic insight into the underlying equity of the brand.

In addition to delineating the four pillars, the model is also used to provide a graphical tool, the "Power Grid," that can help marketers understand the equity position of the brands over time. The Power Grid is a 2x2 layout where Brand Strength is the Y, or vertical axis, and Brand Stature is the X, or horizontal axis. Brand Strength, composed of the Energized Differentiation and Relevance pillars, is an indicator of the future potential of the brand. Brand stature, composed of the Esteem and Knowledge pillars, is an indicator of current brand status. Both dimensions can have a high and low score, and thus four quadrants can be computed.

Brands that are low on both dimensions (such as lululemon, foursquare, and Athlete's Foot) are labeled as new, unfocused, or unknown brands. Brands with high Brand Strength but low Brand Stature (Pom, Fage, or Nespresso) are labeled Niche brands. Those high on both dimensions (IKEA, Visa, Google, Coca-Cola, and Macy's) are labeled Leadership brands. And finally brands that are high on Brand Stature but low on Brand Strength are Commodity, or Eroded, brands. This category includes *TV Guide*, Sprint, Blockbuster, and Spam.)

Brands in the different quadrants must have different strategies to succeed. Leadership brands have to maximize their profit margins and maintain high volume. Niche brands should maximize the return on capital. New brands should be working to develop their potential, and Commodity, or Eroded, brands need to maximize transactions. The four quadrants can also be linked to financial performance and brand-value metrics.

Since the BAV database is longitudinal, a brand's Power Grid coordinates can be plotted over time to provide diagnostic information about the brand's health. For example, the Power Grid metrics for Blockbuster showed the brand holding a strong leadership position in 2001 and then, year by year, declining toward the Eroded brand quadrant, which it hit in 2010. Thus, the Power Grid metrics provided a leading indicator of the problem before it became crystal clear in the marketplace. Netflix, by contrast, showed a very different pattern. In 2005, Netflix was in the Niche quadrant, and moved to the Leadership quadrant in 2006, and then slowly moving up in that quadrant to occupy a strong position by 2011. (It was this strong position that was undermined by the CEO miscalculation later in 2011.) The Power Grid can also be used to plot the movement of a "star" brand. iTunes was in the New brand quadrant in 2005 and moved to the Leadership quadrant by 2007, and continued to move up to a Super Leadership position by 2011.

In summary, the BAV model (including both the Pillars of Brand Health and the Power Grid) is another way to measure the value of brands. The BAV model can provide leading and lagging indicators and can tie these metrics to financial performance data. The Brand Strength, or Energized Differentiation and Relevance metrics, provides leading indicators of brand health and are predictive of a brand's potential. The Brand Stature, or Esteem and Knowledge measures, are lagging indicators and provide a measure of the brand's past performance.

Figure 4.1
Four Pillars Assess Brand Health, Development, Momentum, and Competitive Advantage

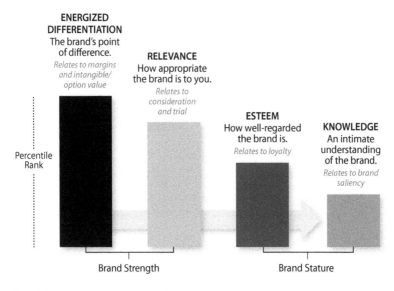

Source: Brand Asset Valuator (BAV) Model

Figure 4.2
The Relationships Among the Four Pillars
Are Key to Understanding the Equity of a Brand

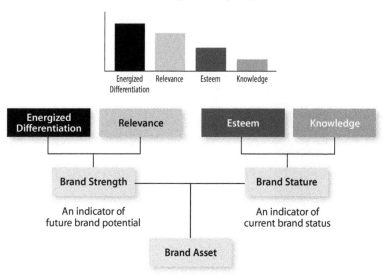

Source: Axes of the Power Grid: Brand Strength and Brand Stature, Brand Asset Valuator (BAV) Model

Using Quantitative Measurment to Guide Action

The advantage of quantitative metrics is that they provide unambiguous indications of the strengths and weaknesses of brands relative to the competition. They also provide evidence of the value of committing resources to developing the brand. These metrics help inspire and evaluate subsequent managerial actions with regard to leveraging and managing the brand asset, issues we discuss next.

Chapter 5

Management of Brands

In this chapter:

- Brand Extensions
- Benefits of Licensing
- Brand Architecture: Strategic System of Brands
- Protecting Value

For a look at just how complicated brand management can get, consider the Marriott Corporation. Its signature brand is the well-known red Marriott Hotels and Resorts trademark, used on all its standard hotels. That brand name and logo also serves as an endorser brand (more about this later) for Courtyard, TownPlace, and SpringHill suites. The Marriott name is further used on the JW Marriott, but quite differently. To signal that JW Marriott is an upscale luxury hotel, the company changes the typeface font and switches the color from red to blue. And the JW Marriott has its own symbol, one that does not appear anywhere else.

With the most iconic luxury brands in its portfolio, the Ritz-Carlton and Bulgari Hotel and Resorts, the Marriott name does not appear at all. For Ritz-Carlton, the perception is that any explicit Marriott linkage would diminish the exclusivity and prestige associated with such a high-end name. Bulgari hotels, for their part, don't seem to exist even in the same lodging universe as other Marriott brands, either physically (Bulgari is a small international chain, with no US presence) or price-wise (the London Bulgari recently offered a "special" two-night stay for £1,560 per night).

The Marriott name can't be found on Renaissance Hotels, either, but for a different reason. Renaissance Hotels cater to a different segment of business travel than those who prefer traditional Marriotts. The standard Marriott appeals to a business traveler concerned with operational excellence, efficiency, and productivity. That traveler likes the familiarity of the chain, knowing it will be exactly the same with each visit. Renaissance Hotels, meanwhile, appeal to business travelers who treasure diversity and who value hotels that mirror the local environment and operate more like a boutique than a hotel chain. Hence, the Marriott name here would be seen as a disadvantage because it would signal sameness rather than diversity.

The Marriott brand name is similarly not used for the Autograph collection of hotels the company operates. The hotels in this collection are a diverse group of individually run hotels, and branding these one-of-a-kinds with the Marriott name would not communicate this sense of individuality and distinctiveness.

Marriott considers all of these hotels as part of a portfolio of options. This portfolio is broad and, it is hoped, provides a lodging option to fit every traveler's needs. In this system, the Marriott brand name varies from the main driver for choice, to an endorsement of quality, to offering little above the individual hotel's own identity. But having all these brands exist in a single portfolio does offer value to the customer because travelers frequent more than one hotel, and they frequent these hotels for different purposes. What's more, wherever they stay within the portfolio, Marriott customers receive loyalty benefits for repeat visits.

Even when a hotel might be stronger without the Marriott brand name, portfolio inclusion offers distinct advantages. Market research, for example, indicates that for loyal Ritz-Carlton consumers, visiting a Ritz-Carlton solves half their hotel needs, and using a different hotel within the system solves the other half. Having a portfolio of hotels that are distinguished by different degrees of "Marriott-ness" allows the traveler to maintain loyalty benefits and still seek variety in his choices. The portfolio also allows for a rich spectrum of price points.

As the Marriott example shows, building brand equity requires a deft management touch. Doing so also represents a substantial investment that needs to be offset by a significant return. As we saw in chapter 4, strong brand equity can deliver profits over and above a comparable unbranded equivalent, but that takes care of today's business, not tomorrow's. Leveraging the investment in existing brand equity for future growth can best be achieved in three ways: (1) brand extensions, (2) licensing, and (3) brand architecture.

The first way to grow revenues is by using the existing brand to introduce new products under that same brand name. This can be done through line extensions within the same category. For example, General Mills used the Cheerios name to introduce new flavors of cereals alongside the original, including Frosted Cheerios, Honey Nut Cheerios, and Apple Cinnamon Cheerios. Another technique involves the use of brand franchise extensions, where an existing brand name is extended to new product categories. Think of how the strong brand name of the ESPN sports television network has been extended to ESPN radio, ESPN magazine, and ESPN.com, where merchandise can be sold.

The second way to grow revenues is through licensing agreements, in which individuals or firms pay for the rights to use existing brand names, logos, and characters of other brands to market their own products. These third parties make and sell products and services under a brand name and pay the company that owns that brand a percentage of the sales in the form of a royalty. For example, Sara Lee Corporation's Hillshire Farm, which makes sausages, licensed the brand name Miller

High Life to produce beer brats. The Crayola brand name has been licensed out to companies that have used it to produce Crayola-brand freezer pops, magnets, and colorful plastic plates. Perry Ellis owns the Nike license to produce Nike swimwear.

The third way to increase the return on investment is to leverage the brand equity of existing products to build new brands for new products. Maximizing relationships among these different brands requires an overarching brand architecture. The optimal brand architecture depends on the characteristics of the market and the firm, but it can be found somewhere between a "house of brands," where each brand in the system is individual and the corporate brand name is not promoted, and a "branded house," where all products are identified to some degree by the corporate brand.

Existing brands can also work in tandem across firms to create a new, hybrid brand through co-branding. For example, Apple and Nike co-branded Sport Kit, a wireless system that allows shoes to talk to an iPod. Similarly, Benjamin Moore partnered with Pottery Barn to create a co-branded color palette of paints for each season. When growth is determined through mergers and/or acquisitions, existing brand names can also be leveraged for the new combined firm.

Brand Extensions

The easiest way to leverage an existing brand name is to use it to introduce a similar product in the same category or a new entrant in a related category. The new product can be a simple line extension—a new flavor, say. Or the existing brand can be used to introduce the same product in a different form (as with Jell-O Pudding Pops) or to call attention to an ingredient in a new product (e.g., when M&M- or Snickers-branded candy pieces are used in icecream desserts). The existing name can also be used for a companion product. Thus Pantene leveraged its equity in shampoo to create a creme rinse or other hair care or beauty products. Product extensions also can build on a distinctive benefit. Consider how Ivory soap, known for its mildness, was extended to Ivory detergent and Ivory dishwashing liquid. Or a firm can try to leverage the status from one product to promote another. The Prada name, for example, has been used to bring prestige across categories ranging from clothing to shoes to purses to fragrances.

Brand extensions can also help delineate tiers within a product line. This is called vertical stretching and can go in either direction, although stretching down is easier than stretching up. Gallo, originally known for its jug wines, provides an example of stretching up, when the brand is used for premium varietal wines. Giorgio Armani, the couture brand, stretches its brand down when it introduces lower-priced Armani brands such as Armani Collezioni, Emporio Armani, Armani Jeans, A/X, and Armani Exchange.

Advantages and disadvantages of brand extension

Brand extensions provide multiple routes for increasing revenues. First, the extensions appeal to different segments and thus bring in new users. Second, the extensions offer variety for existing users, increasing purchases per user. Brand extensions have the potential to expand the retail shelf space, which can block competition and thus bring in additional sales.

The extensions can be used within and across channels to strengthen the relationship between the manufacturer and the retailer, which can lead to strategic advantages in the marketing process. For example, electronics and appliance retailers frequently ask manufacturers for their own brands and/ or model numbers so that they can carry exclusive offerings. This helps control price comparisons across channels. Doing so also thwarts a practice mentioned earlier—showrooming, where people test out products in a physical store at one retailer and purchase the product online from a discount source. Finally, stretching the brand up and down across a broad range of price points satisfies customers who have different budget constraints and price sensitivities.

Brand extensions also have cost advantages. Extending an existing name makes the introduction of new products or new lines less expensive because it leverages existing awareness and customers can instantly identify the new product advantages. Promotions, messaging, and communications strategies become more efficient because several line extensions can be promoted within the same message. Even for individual product advertising, there are advantages, because one line can indirectly advertise the other via the common name. New-product extensions help revitalize a brand by adding a modern element or diversifying and stretching brand meanings.

The caveat: Brand extensions that are not well managed undermine brand equity. If the extension is not consistent with the original brand, it can confuse or frustrate the customer and dilute or even destroy the original meanings. Retailers may balk at the additional lines and not provide the needed shelf space. New extensions also sometimes cannibalize the originals, as happened with Miller Lite. The light version of the original Miller High Life beer, Miller Lite was a very successful extension in terms of its own revenues, but its very success undermined the equity in the original because consumers thought it had a less hearty taste. Adding too many extensions threatens to dilute a brand, making it lose its competitive advantages.

The issue of fit

Although no strategy for developing good brand extensions is foolproof, the likelihood of a disaster can be mitigated. In order to develop a good brand extension, the associations with the original brand name must fit the new product. For example, extending the Oreo name to shoes would make no sense, while extending the name to ice cream did prove profitable, because the associations with Oreos fit with the icecream category. Similarly, where Ralph Lauren might work well with shoes, it would add little benefit to a new icecream product.

Extending a brand name to a new product that does not offer some superior benefit relative to the competitors in the category is also more likely to dilute brand-equity value than to grow it. Finally, even if the associations with the original brand name do link to the new category, the results may not be desirable. Campbell decided against putting its brand name on tomato sauce after consumers indicated in testing that they thought the tomato sauce would be watery.

The best brand extensions use associations from the existing brand that appropriately fit the new category. Very strong extensions can similarly add value back to the original brand. For example, Burberry extends its brand name from the iconic raincoats to accessories and clothing lines. The Burberry name adds value to these new lines, and in return, having a full line underneath the Burberry brand brings a contemporary perspective back to the original brand. One of the most successful products in this extension strategy was the Burberry bathing suit, which combines the classical quality of the original brand with sexy, provocative fashion. Thus extensions keep the brand fresh, modern, and relevant.

Brands can also use extensions to stretch the original name even further and thus increase its value. The name Weight Watchers originally appeared only on diet centers. Then the companysuccessfully extended its name by attaching it to low-calorie foods sold in grocery stores. Now Weight Watchers is associated with weight loss, weight maintenance, and a whole calorie-conscious lifestyle.

The best way to determine appropriate extensions is through market testing to explore the fit and power of the brand in a new category. Ensuring that the brand name fits the new product may not be a straightforward application of the original associations, either. The meaning of associations in one category can change when they are applied in a new category. Inappropriate extensions can fail in many ways. They just may not work; they may destroy the original equity. Or overuse may dilute the brand power. Extensive marketing research can mitigate these risks. And it never makes sense either to extend a weak brand or to use a strong brand name on a weak product.

Benefits of Licensing

Another way to leverage the investment in building brand equity is to sell the rights to the trademark to a third party, or licensee. The licensor receives royalties for use of the trademark, and is thus provided a stream of revenues without incurring any more costs. Sometimes the additional goods sold by the licensee help improve the product experience for the original brand. For example, Apple licensed the iPod brand name to makers of accessory products, and these other companies made ancillary items such as cases or sound systems, which ultimately improved the experience of the iPod without forcing Apple to move away from its core strengths.

As just mentioned, it may be advantageous for the brand to be extended into new categories, both to stretch the brand and/or to keep it relevant. This may require venturing into areas in which the firm lacks expertise. In such instances, a firm can license its brand to another entity with product expertise in the new category. Witness how P&G licensed its Mr. Clean brand to Magla to produce cleaning accessories under the Mr. Clean brand, thus making Mr. Clean a cleaning system, rather than a single product.

Advantages for the licensee

A licensee gets to use a proven brand name without having to invest or risk nearly as much as it would if it were building a name from scratch. This can mean significant time advantages in going to market. Plus, licensing a strong name should allow the licensee to charge a price premium for the product.

Licensing can build a reputation for a designer or a celebrity name very quickly. This approach is common in the fashion industry. Typically, a designer signs a licensing contract with a third-party manufacturer to produce various products under the designer's name. In this way, a designer can quickly turn out a large product line, gain increased brand awareness through distribution of these products, and earn a royalty every time an item bearing his name is sold.

The Iconix Brand Group played this game from the business side. It purchased many licenses with in a short time, including Candie's, the teen shoe brand, and Joe Boxer, the trendy underwear brand. Iconix then made licensing deals directly with the retailers, giving them exclusivity and thus more control over the products than is normally the case. Candie's, for example, is available only at Kohl's, and Joe Boxer is exclusive to Sears.

Concerns over too much licensing

Although licensing contracts can be very profitable for all parties involved, the strategy does entail numerous risks. Once a firm sells the rights to use its trademark to another organization, the original firm loses control. A licensee might manufacture products that are not up to the brand's standards or may group too many products or services under the brand name, thus diluting its value. When this happens, the original firm may try to buy back the rights so that it has more control. This was the case when Ralph Lauren sold the licensing rights to its Polo

Jeans Co. name to Jones Apparel. Four months later, the Ralph Lauren Corporation got the rights back because it believed that the brand had been overpromoted and overdistributed, thus threatening the whole brand franchise. Not only was there a problem with the jeans that Jones was producing under the Polo name, but by selling the license for that brand to Jones, Ralph Lauren itself was precluded from entering the premium denim market—which had, in the meantime, become very lucrative.

Brand Architecture: Strategic Systems of Brands

There is a huge opportunity to leverage the strength of a strong master brand toward developing a whole system of brand names in new categories and new markets. Doing this strategically requires a framework for understanding how the different brands should interact.

David Aaker—professor emeritus at University of California, Berkeley, and self-proclaimed "branding guru"—coined the term "brand architecture" to describe this process. Just as a physical house has different rooms, with each one serving a unique purpose but all working together to create a coherent living structure, so should brands work together, with each having a different function within the framework. The key is to make sure that each brand's identity is maintained even as one brand's identity is being leveraged to aid another's.

This is a tricky process, because if not done well, the result can be muddled brand positioning rather than augmented value. Many strategic issues go into determining the exact structure of the system, including both the breadth and depth of product mix (how many product lines should be included within the system and how many variants should be included within each product line).

In evaluating the merits of a particular type of brand architecture, four goals should be kept in mind. The first is overall clarity both of the system as a whole and of each brand. Each brand's positioning must be simple, and the relationships among brands must be clear. The second goal is synergy; while each brand must work by itself, in order for a system to be justified the whole must be bigger than the sum of the parts. In other words, if there is not some additional value in linking one brand to another, there's no point in joining them. A third goal of a good system is leverage. The point of bringing brands together is to be able to leverage some of the equity of one brand to be used by another in the system. Finally, all brands in the system must be strong. The system is only as strong as its weakest link.

Figure 5.1
Brand Relationship Spectrum

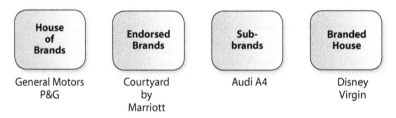

House of Brands	Endorsed Brands	Sub-brands	Branded House
General Motors P&G	Courtyard by Marriott	Audi A4	Disney Virgin

Source: Adapted from *Brand Leadership,* by David A. Aaker and Erich Joachimsthaler. Copyright © 2000 by David A. Aaker and Erich Joachimsthaler.

House of brands versus branded house

Aaker proposed that brand systems should range from a house of brands portfolio to a branded house portfolio. With a house of brands, each brand has a separate identity and the over-riding connector is not made explicitly public. General Motors is a house of brands that including Cadillac, Buick, and Chevrolet. Similarly, P&G is a house of brands that includes Tide, Ivory, and Crest, none of which is obviously linked to the P&G corporate brand in its packaging or advertising. This is particularly true in the United States. In some other markets, P&G does link these product names back to the corporate brand.

P&G uses more corporate branding when doing business outside the United States because other nations value the corporate brand more. For example, in Japan, corporate branding is very strong—think Panasonic and Sony, both of which are branded with their corporate name. In other countries, the presence of the corporate brand signifies certain values and social responsibilities. In the United States, although this trend is changing, P&G found great benefit in promoting a diversity of brands, whose individual identities might be hampered by being too closely linked.

A branded house is the opposite of a house of brands. In a branded house, all the brands in the system carry the over-arching corporate brand name globally. Disney and Virgin—to cite two high-profile examples—are both branded houses.

In between are endorsed brands—closer to a house of brands but with each of these new brand names endorsed by the corporate brand. Courtyard by Marriott is an instance where the corporate brand of Marriott gives credibility to the new Courtyard brand. Eventually, this hotel chain will likely be known just as Courtyard, once the Marriott endorser brand has achieved its goal. A sub-brand, closer to the branded-house concept, is a new-brand line created under the corporate brand, such as the Audi A4, but where the new brand, A4, will likely never stand on its own.

The advantage of the house-of-brands approach is that these new brands have unique identities and can therefore cater to radically different market segments. Having separate brands also minimizes any negative contamination. If a brand disaster happens to one brand in the house, the fallout should be minimal on the other brands. A house of brands can also increase shelf space in a retail environment or in a particular locale. If the optimal location for hotels is close to an airport, a hotel chain probably shouldn't put up several hotels with the exact same name very close to one another. Marriott solves this problem by having several endorsed brands, such as Courtyard, SpringHill Suites, and TownPlace Suites, that can be located close to one another without appearing to saturate the market. A house of brands also provides more options for variety seekers. Still a house of brands does have its disadvantages. For one, it is expensive to develop and maintain many separate identities. Further, these brands often compete with one another and thus could be cannibalizing sales, rather than building the overall category. Because of these cost disadvantages, the trend is toward more consolidated efforts—a move toward the branded house and away from the house-of-brands concept.

Some strategic points to consider when thinking about brand architecture are: when to create a new name versus just keeping the old name on the extension; if it's a new name should it be a sub-brand, an endorsed brand, or a distinct new entity; and how extensively the overall corporate brand name should be used in messaging and packaging.

Subtle variations exist among these categories of branding options. A brand system does not have to impose a universal strategy; the system can have a blend of endorsed brands, sub-brands, and examples in between. Consider Kraft food products. The question here is how prominent the Kraft corporate name should be on each of the products. Some products are branded only by the master brand—Kraft cheese, Kraft Barbecue Sauce, and Kraft Mayonnaise. Other brands, such as Kraft Minute Rice and Kraft Stovetop Stuffing, have a strong Kraft endorsement but still have their own name. Then there are cases where Kraft is an endorser brand but is used only minimally, such as for Philadelphia Cream Cheese or Velveeta. With still other brands such as Oscar Mayer and Cool Whip, the Kraft endorsement is virtually nonexistent. In this system, Kraft has to decide how much value the corporate name would add to the product and, based on that understanding, whether to augment and promote the corporate name or to silence it.

Mergers and acquisitions

Another situation that requires brands to work in sync to create a new entity is when corporations merge or one corporation acquires another. What happens then to the brand names involved? There are probably as many answers as there are examples, and in each case, market research is required to determine whether the brand names should be combined equally, whether one should subsume the other, or whether a new name that somehow combines the entities should be created.

Consider the merger of US Trust and Bank of America. The question was what to brand the private banking business. Management had decided that the private banking sides of both firms should be merged under one brand name, due to the cost of maintaining the brands separately, but this was easier said than done. The two private banking brands had very different identities in the marketplace. US Trust was on the A list of top five private wealth brands, along with Bessemer, Goldman Sachs, Northern Trust, and J.P. Morgan. Bank of America Private Bank did not score as high, but it was a more familiar brand name, a much bigger organization, with five times the number of relationships and twice as many assets under administration as US Trust, and was far more global. BofA also was perceived to have more significant resources.

The final decision was that the US Trust brand name should lead, as it telegraphed wealth management expertise and established credibility, but that the Bank of America identity should be used as an endorser brand (in small type below the main branding) to communicate the larger enterprise strengths.

The final new logo—with the US Trust logo large and the Bank of America name underneath, much smaller—featured the US Trust colors of black and white (rather than the red, white, and blue Bank of America colors), but Bank of America's red-white-and-blue flag logo was also used.

Each specific merger or acquisition requires unique decisions, but all of them share common market research questions. What is the strength of each brand name and its associations? Why do customers choose each brand, and which brand has the largest potential to increase future business? Which brand will result in a larger customer migration if the brand is compromised? What is the elasticity of brand loyalty for each of the brands? Finally, at the graphic level, can the logos and colors work together?

Figuring out how old and new brands can work together to create new value is especially complicated when considered globally. In this case, all these research questions and strategies have to be evaluated with regard to each market and culture. One famous example of a merger that failed partly because the company could not reconcile all the cultural differences, including language and styles, was the merger between Daimler-Benz and Chrysler. The German company, Daimler-Benz, was known for high-quality German engineering performance and centralized processes and decision making. Its Mercedes-Benz brand was a premium, luxury brand. The American Chrysler Co., for its part, had a culture of flexibility and more "can do" American ingenuity. Its car brands (Chrysler, Dodge, Plymouth, and Jeep) were prevalent in blue-collar communities. The managerial cultures as well as the conflicting brand values ended up being irreconcilable, and eventually the merger dissolved. A post-merger analysis revealed that the conflicting cultures led to an inability to achieve the desired synergies and ultimately the collapse of the arrangement.

A cross-border merger of big brands that appears to have been more successful was Belgian InBev's acquisition of the American Anheuser-Busch company, maker of Budweiser beer. Right from the beginning, InBev pledged to preserve Anheuser's American heritage. In fact, the American culture is a critical aspect of the marketing campaign as Budweiser beer attempts to go global.

Protecting Value

To protect the heavy investment in global branding and to leverage that outlay for growth, brand managers need to keep two dimensions first and foremost in their minds.

1. **The number of brand names.** Are the existing ones even relevant? If they are, do they need a new extension to stretch their meaning or to keep them contemporary? Then the question is how to reap as much value out of each brand name as possible. For example, can they be used to develop new brands?
2. **The breadth of the product categories.** Here, managers need to concern themselves with whether the growth of the business should be within a category or across several categories. When thinking about developing new brands, the key strategic questions involve how brands can work together synergistically to create a powerful brand architecture.

In the last chapter, I explore how all these branding strategies can be communicated through graphic elements and naming strategies. I also talk about the importance of keeping a brand relevant and modern, and what a manager can do if a brand needs to be repositioned.

Chapter 6

Effective Brand Communications and Repositioning Strategies

In this chapter:

• Brand Names
• Use of Celebrities with Brands
• Cause Marketing
• Repositioning a Brand

For a brand to exist, it needs a name. Historically, many of the classic iconic brands are family names. Ford, Levi Strauss and Co., Estée Lauder, Ralph Lauren, RJ Reynolds, Wrigley, Yale, Westinghouse, Marriott, Woolworth's, and Michelin all bear the names of their founders. But a birth or given name might not be the best choice for creating a memorable brand.

Who, for example, has ever heard of Stefani Joanne Angelina Germanotta? Yet both *Fast Company* and the *Wall Street Journal* have called her one of the most exciting brand phenoms of recent times, not for her birth name, to be sure, but for her creative brand name: Lady Gaga.

Needless to say, Lady Gaga is an accomplished performer, but she is also a branding genius, and that genius begins with the selection of her brand name. She has even branded her devoted set of fans—her "little monsters"—and they follow her tantalizing social media communiqués religiously and in vast numbers: 47 million Facebook fans and more than 18 million Twitter followers, and the numbers are growing.

Why is the Lady Gaga name so great? It's memorable and distinctive. She uses the paradoxical pairing of the slangy "gaga" (as in head-over-heels infatuated) with the classic, elegant title of "lady." And as with any strong communications plan, her brand has unique elements: icons, gimmicks, costumes, and vaudeville performances to build and develop her image.

Lady Gaga knows the power of her brand name, and she vigilantly protects it against copycats who might undermine her uniqueness. Case in point: She sued and successfully obtained an injunction against the Moshi Monsters singer Lady Goo Goo, a product of a children's social network site that was parodying her name and threatening her legitimacy.

Brand Names

Many different types of brand names can be chosen if you are starting from a blank slate. One option is to use a combination of your name and a description of a product—"Walmart" worked pretty well for Sam Walton. The name can have some kind of poetic or literary derivation that serves as an inspiration. The Greek goddess of victory inspired the Nike name, and the swoosh, an abstraction of a wing, symbolizes her flight. The name can represent attributes or symbolism of the brand—"Volkswagen" means "people's car" in German; "Vodafone" is a combination of "voice," "data," and "telephone"—or it can be a conglomeration of ideas as in "Verizon," which mixes *veritas* (Latin for "truth") and "horizon." The name can also be descriptive as is the case of "Lean Cuisine," "Weight Watchers," "Rent-a-Wreck," and "7-Eleven" (the hours the stores were originally open). Or it can be a happy mistake. Google was originally meant to be "Googol" (10 raised to the hundredth power), but in creating the original Internet domain name, someone misspelled "Googol," and the rest is history.

Criteria to consider

In thinking about the best name, several criteria should be considered. First, the name should be easily pronounced and remembered. Although some brands have overcome this handicap—Geico (originally Government Employees Insurance Company) comes to mind, with its clever gecko commercials, or Aflac (American Family Life Assurance Company), with its squawking duck—it's clearly better not to have to pay to explain how to pronounce the brand name correctly! But if the brand is too familiar or similar to others pursuing the same customers—State Farm and All State, or Goodyear and Goodrich—there are obvious disadvantages as well.

A brand name should be able to be trademarked and thus not copied. Ensure that a domain name on the web can be obtained, and that the name can be easily recalled and associated with the brand, and readily searchable. It also pays to check whether Facebook or other social networking sites are using the name or similar names. Also check that the name works globally and does not mean something unfavorable in another language.

Translating the brand name into other languages can be an issue, particularly when the alphabets are different. Many Western brands have chosen to keep their Western logo rather than translate it into another language. Entering the Chinese market is particularly interesting, because it's important that if a brand is translated into Chinese characters that the characters have a meaning consistent with the brand. Making a literal translation or trying to mimic the sounds without understanding the additional meanings of the characters could create problems. Similar sounds can be associated with different Chinese characters, all of which have very different meanings. Perhaps the most famous mishap here was for Coca-Cola, which translated its brand into Chinese characters that sounded like its English name, but the characters actually read "bite the wax tadpole." Obviously not the best marketing message! Coke had to redo its whole trademark process to get it right the next time.

A name must deliver on all the strategic advantages that a good brand should offer—something distinctive, appealing, and meaningful, perhaps with visual or verbal imagery associated with it. Apple is a very strong brand name for many, many reasons, but the striking imagery and simplicity don't hurt. Brands that evoke emotions such as joy can likewise be more memorable.

A brand also needs to be able to grow with the company and product line, and be stretchable enough to include possible brand extensions. Boston Chicken as a brand name was very limiting, and it was eventually changed for that very reason to Boston Market. Dunkin' Donuts is similarly grappling with its legacy name. Starbucks Coffee recently dropped first the word "Coffee," then the word "Starbucks" itself from its logo on its coffee mugs as it prepared to go international and stretch across many different product categories. In general, brand names that are too associated with a single product or specific attribute may not be as flexible or adaptive as they should be.

Finally, it's important to anticipate changing times and values. "Kentucky Fried Chicken" became dated and limiting—hence, its migration to KFC. "Twentieth Century–Fox" is obviously so last century! But brand names like "Virgin" that are fun and fresh and not tied to a specific product category can become very valuable, as they expand across many categories and countries.

Other brand elements

Once the name has been chosen, other brand elements can be employed to create a design personality. The logo typeface font is a critical decision, as is the choice of a symbol or brand character to be associated with the name. The goal here: a logo that draws attention, reinforces brand associations, and can transfer globally. Carefully chosen symbols and characters can imbue the name with deeper meaning and reinforce critical associations, but these same symbols and characters can be misinterpreted or, again, become dated. The old P&G symbol, which showed an old bearded man looking over 13 stars, was rumored to have satanic connections. P&G continuously denied the allegations, but the rumors persisted. Finally, in the 1990s, P&G changed the corporate logo to a blue scripted P&G wordmark. Slogans and jingles can convey additional nuanced meanings, but the may be difficult to translate. Whatever elements are eventually chosen, they must work together and be used consistently.

If the brand is a physical product, some of the distinctiveness can come through the packaging. Absolut Vodka differentiated itself in a crowded premium vodka category through its unusual bottle shape—a short neck instead of the more typical long-necked version. The bottle shape was such an important aspect of the brand that it was featured in creative ways for more than 10 years in Absolut's well-known print ad campaigns.

Similarly, the Heinz ketchup bottle shape is so much a part of the brand and so iconic that it is featured in the Smithsonian Museum. The irony of the Heinz bottle is that although it is differentiating, its shape makes it difficult to dispense the ketchup. Heinz tried to turn that difficulty into an advantage by featuring "ketchup races" in its advertising, maintaining that the slowest ketchup out of the bottle when the bottles were turned upside down was the thickest, richest-flavored product.

Color

Logo color is one of the first things consumers notice about a brand and one of the elements that lingers longest in memory. The ultimate goal is to own a color within the category—

Tiffany's light blue, say, and Mary Kay's pink. Some colors are so associated with a brand that just showing the color within a category communicates the brand. UPS's brown trucks and uniforms differentiate the company sufficiently even if the name is not observed.

Colors are defined on two axes, affect and arousal. High-arousal colors such as red, yellow, and orange are attention getting, while low-arousal colors such as blue and green are considered calming. The affect dimension can differ by culture and country. In the United States, blue is a well-liked color, while in India orange is valued. The Chinese find red very appealing and blue to be cold. Gold and silver can be used to communicate prestige, whereas pale pink and lavender denote fragility. Color preferences differ by product class as well. Red, blue, and black are preferred colors in clothing, while beige and browns are appealing in home furnishing. Colors also can go in and out of style. Witness the trend away from blues and toward yellows.

The target user should always be considered when it's time to choose a brand's color, because color preferences differ across demographic variables. For example, children are drawn to neon colors, while older people like more muted browns and grays. Consideration should also be given to how the color plays in different contexts. How does it look online versus in a store? Does the color work on white? How will scale affect the color? In some cases, a company can legally protect the use of a color within a category, which presents another factor to consider.

Use of Celebrities with Brands

The intense media fascination with celebrities means that they can become a brand in and of themselves, as with Lady Gaga. Kim Kardashian has turned her celebrity brand into a multiline business, leveraging various reality shows and Twitter feeds to drum up attention for her Kardashian Kollection of new lingerie and her new fragrance. Or celebrities can be used effectively to endorse brand meanings and affiliation.

Celebrities augment brand equity in two important ways. First, a celebrity spokesperson can provide credibility. In this case, the effectiveness of the association of a celebrity with a brand depends on the celebrity's perceived expertise or trustworthiness. Thus, people may buy Martha Stewart cookware because of Stewart's expertise in the kitchen. Celebrities also can positively sway connection with a brand through what is known as source attractiveness, in which the celebrity's likeability and familiarity are the key factors. People buy Jennifer Lopez fragrance because Lopez is sexy and attractive, not because they think she is an expert at identifying scents.

The effectiveness of a celebrity endorser or a celebrity as a brand in and of itself is also a function of the fit of the celebrity either with the target audience or with the product. Research has shown that a celebrity has positive and negative associations. When the product is a good match with the celebrity identity, positive associations transfer over to the brand. Conversely, if the product is not a good match, negative associations are likely to transfer from the celebrity to the brand.

Of course, the biggest risk with the use of celebrities to promote or create a brand is that celebrities are human. If their life takes a scandalous turn, those negative associations can affect the brand image. Tiger Woods and Lance Armstrong are famous recent examples. At one time both were two of the most successful celebrity endorsers. Tiger's credibility as a world-class athlete helped build Nike brand equity for golf products, while his attractiveness as a successful achiever helped create positive associations with nongolf products such as Accenture or Tag watches. However, as soon as his extramarital affairs came to light, companies with nongolf associations were quick to drop him, while golf-related brands such as Nike kept up the affiliation. For Armstrong, when the doping evidence became overwhelming, sponsors quickly dropped him.

In addition to providing instant market visibility, celebrities can be very effective at communicating brand values if there is a strong association between the celebrity and the brand, but unless the celebrity is the brand, the celebrity should not overshadow a product. The brand values and meanings must be communicated over and above the celebrity affiliation.

Cause Marketing

Many brands have recently realized the importance of not only appealing to their own customers and employees but also accepting the responsibility of contributing to society. Brands have adopted specific causes and then, through either promotions or sponsorships, provided support for the charity or nonprofit agency. Think of Dressbarn's association with the American Cancer Society's Relay for Life, or Avon and *Glamour* magazine's support for breast cancer awareness, or NBC and ABC's support for teacher recruitment and antidrug campaigns. These partnerships are mutually beneficial. The brand builds awareness for the cause and monetary contributions by committing a certain percentage of sales to whatever the cause is backing. Simultaneously, affiliation with a cause can improve brand perceptions and emotions toward the brand.

Not to undermine the genuine altruistic and social responsibility goals of a corporation in connecting with a cause, but there are also genuine branding benefits. All things being equal, consumers will certainly value corporations that are socially responsible over those just out to make a buck. That's especially true when the causes fit the interests of the firm and when the altruism seems to be consistent with self-interest, but if the connection appears inauthentic or opportunistic, the "good Samaritan" approach can backfire.

Look at KFC's connection with the Susan G. Komen Foundation during National Breast Cancer Awareness Month in 2010. KFC sold "Buckets for the Cure," with a portion of the revenues going to the foundation. Sounds generous, to be sure, but breast cancer supporters found this a disingenuous campaign, arguing that eating fatty foods was inconsistent with healthy living. Petitions called "What the cluck?" were circulated, encouraging Komen to drop the connection.

When the values in support of the cause are built directly into the fabric of the company from the start, the connection is even more authentic. For example, from its beginnings, Ben & Jerry's valued social responsibility and giving back to the community. Ben & Jerry's website identifies three social mission goals: (1) further the cause of peace and justice, (2) make ice cream that's aligned with our values, and (3) take the lead promoting global sustainable dairy practices. That these goals have been in place from the start and that there are detailed and comprehensive strategies and business practices to implement them gives the brand very strong credibility. Even when Unilever ultimately acquired the brand, the company mantra was so pure that it survived the transition from its roots as a small, personalized company to ownership by a huge corporation.

Association with a cause can also polarize a customer base as Chick-fil-A discovered when its president and COO, Dan Cathy, expressed his opinions against same-sex marriage. Predictably, very strong reactions emerged on both sides of the issues. Some public officials and LGBT political activists expressed outrage over the COO and his company and staged protests against the restaurants. Supporters of the COO countered with an unofficial "Chick-fil-A Appreciation Day." Certainly Chick-fil-A lost some customers with the political stance, but the statement of values reinforced the loyalty of others. Most corporate brands choose to avoid this kind of controversy, but it is interesting to observe public reaction when a company executive speaks out.

Repositioning a Brand

Brand meanings and communications strategies must be actively managed over time, or brands can lose their way. Sometimes old associations are no longer relevant, either because the product is dated, as with Kodak photographic film, or because the associations with the brand have become stodgy or old-fashioned, as happened with Oldsmobile. In these situations, communications strategies can be used to reposition the brand. Repositioning a brand requires changing consumers' attitudes toward it, but that can be a high bar to clear. Studies of attitude change have shown that there is a basic drive to maintain consistency. People do not like dissonance, and they do what they can, including rationalization, to resolve the dissonance. For example, many people who eat high-calorie food while on vacation will convince themselves that calories do not count in such circumstances. Instead of employing common sense, they interpret the data around them in a way that is consistent with their existing beliefs and desires, and—critically—their behaviors at the moment.

With regard to repositioning brands, this drive for consistency makes it difficult to change people's minds once they have experienced a bad brand image. The most famous example of this is the advertising strategy that Oldsmobile used in the hope of modernizing people's perceptions of its cars. Many young people thought of Oldsmobile as a car their fathers drove. When Oldsmobile tried to create advertising that presented its cars instead as youthful and exciting, consumers experienced cognitive dissonance because they could not associate something young and exciting with their dads. To achieve consistency, they reinterpreted the ads, regardless of content, as showing nonexciting cars. The association between the cars and the older generation was too strong—even good advertising and improved products could not change the perceptions. The fact that the car was named OLDsmobile obviously did not help the situation. Furthermore, the famous advertising tagline "This is not your father's Oldsmobile" both failed to change people's minds and reinforced beliefs about the stodginess of the cars. In the end, General Motors removed the cars from the marketplace, in spite of the strong brand awareness, because of the persistency of these beliefs.

The Oldsmobile example shows that once beliefs become embedded in people's minds, repositioning the brand can be nearly impossible. The key is to slowly but steadily evolve the brand to keep it fresh and modern. Symbols can be continually updated. Mr. Clean, Betty Crocker, and Charlie the Tuna are historically associated with famous brands, but they've all undergone gradual makeovers to keep the associations fresh. Continuous modernization of the packaging and logo can also help.

Another way to keep the brand dynamic is to change the slogans on a regular basis. Burger King has regularly changed its slogan as it tries to communicate its changing brand positioning strategies. It moved from a product-focused strategy ("Home of the Whopper") in the early 1950s, through the 1980s ("We know how burgers should be"), to value in the 1990s ("Get your burger's worth"), to clever customer-focused social media campaigns aimed at attracting its target segment in the 2000s, including the hugely successful viral "Subservient Chicken" campaign, which symbolized the company's "Have it your way" slogan.

As mentioned in chapter 5, brand extensions can help keep the brand rejuvenated. Finally, brand sponsorships can help bring in new segments of consumers by increasing awareness. Budweiser beer keeps up its youthful connections by sponsoring events such as concerts and festivals.

Continual attention to positioning and communications strategies can keep a brand contemporary, but the changes must be steady and consistent, and they must build upon the core meanings and heritage of the brand. If the brand has been allowed to grow stale, gradual changes and updating may not be sufficient to keep it fresh. In that case, the only chance may be to try a silver bullet strategy. The idea here is to do something so radical that it forces consumers to rethink their beliefs about a brand.

Hush Puppies shoes were designed to be comfortable and casual. The brand was very successful at persuading people to buy the shoes initially, but getting them to repurchase was difficult. People thought of them as slippers, house shoes that lasted forever. To encourage repurchase, Hush Puppies changed the colors of the shoes from browns, beiges, and neutrals to neon colors. This drastic change instantly altered the perception of the shoes as house slippers to a trendy accessory, and thus encouraged repurchase. By dramatically transforming existing beliefs, Hush Puppies broke out of its mold. This kind of strategy is risky and may not always work, but if the brand is approaching terminal staleness, a last-resort strategy may be needed.

Using brand elements to communicate strategy

As mentioned in chapter 5, managing systems of brands is complicated and requires marketing research and strategic analysis in order to maximize growth and the potential for revenue. Once these decisions are made, the brand elements just discussed can be used effectively to communicate the final results to consumers.

An example: Deutsche Post World Net, the German post office, purchased three companies—DHL, Danzas, and Postbank—in its quest to become a general mail, express mail, logistics, and finance company. The decision was made to connect the various companies under a recognizable corporate brand name. But how to do it?

Deutsche Post, the purchasing company, had a very strong, proud German culture and was very well known in its home country. DHL, on the other hand, was originally an American company and sported a quite different, Wild West culture, but it also had the highest worldwide reputation among all the brands in the new portfolio.

The logos and colors of the two brands were also far apart. DHL's brand colors were red and white, while Deutsche Post's logo was black on a yellow background.

In the end, the decision was made to unite the company under the smaller and better-known DHL brand, but the brand elements were creatively combined to retain remnants of the original corporate history and culture while also creatively reflecting the new corporate name. The new logo featured the DHL trademark, but on Deutsche Post's yellow background, rather than on the original white. New trucks were painted Deutsche Post bright yellow, but with the new DHL logo. The final effect was simultaneously to acknowledge the past, signal the merger of the brands, and accentuate the new culture of the corporate group—an impressive hat trick!

Conclusion

To paraphrase David Ogilvy, the advertising mastermind, anybody can put a product on sale, but it takes real genius to create a global brand. Strong global brands have distinctive universal meanings that offer value to consumers everywhere. Recently McDonald's, best known for its Big Mac and "all-beef patties," announced that two new restaurants in northern India would serve only vegetarian food, the first in the chain's long history. The McDonald's brand is definitely global, as is its "I'm lovin' it" brand slogan and famous Golden Arches, but the menus, the distribution, and even the advertising are obviously tailored to the local environment.

As Coca-Cola learned from its famous disaster with New Coke, the brand name has value over and above any product attributes, and the best brands have strong long-term relationships with their customers. Consumers own the brand, and when so motivated, they can become its very best advocate. Of course, it's a double-edged sword: one false step, and the consequences instantly reverberate around the world through social media tools.

Strong brands are an important part of why people buy. But, for consumers, the purchase process is not simply buy or don't buy the next pair of Ferragamo shoes. There are multiple touch points along the path to purchase where a brand can meaningfully influence customers' perceptions and loyalties. From the living stage through planning, shopping, and experiencing, brands have become ubiquitous parts of our lives both online and off.

Strong emotional attachment describes the way customers feel about the best global brands. And in today's world, where stalwart financial advisers are charged with generating Ponzi schemes, and Harvard students are accused of cheating, brands that are authentic and can be completely trusted are tremendous differentiators. As BAV reports, trust is now "the new black" in branding strategies.

Yes, the brand asset is one of the most important investments a firm has, but none of its power is accidental. Brands have to be actively managed and supported. Strong brands have better positioning and richer brand experiences than other weaker brands in their competitive contexts. These brand meanings also have to be dynamic in that they keep pace with changing marketing environments. Finally, good brand positioning requires making choices—deciding what a brand is and, more important, what it is not.

The only way to really understand brand value from the customer perspective is through careful measurement. Qualitative measurement can provide a lens into consumers' minds and explore what they think and feel, rather than what they may be prone to reveal. Techniques such as ZMET, which probes the deep underlying metaphors surrounding purchase; the Implicit Association Test, which uncovers implicit associations as opposed to explicitly stated attitudes; and ethnography, which explores the culture surrounding the brand use, are a few of the creative tools that progressive brand managers can use.

Quantitative measurement allows a more precise appreciation for long-term value of the brand as well as revenue-generating opportunities. Standard marketing surveys help determine levels of brand awareness, brand attitudes, and customer satisfaction. And using customer analytics on behavioral data that's been generated through retail scanners or through web browsing may provide insights into customer and brand loyalty.

As with any investment, strong brands can be leveraged to create additional growth potential. Brand and category extensions often reduce the cost of introducing new products and revitalize the brand. Brand systems built on a strong driver brand have the ability to reach into new, lucrative markets and customer segments. Licensing, if not overused, can produce another revenue source. Strategic co-branding and brand endorsements can create new, hybrid brands that may eventually have revenue streams of their own. Mergers and acquisitions provide another opportunity for creativity and resourcefulness in brand management.

Finally, there are the tactical and design issues that must be considered for creating names and logos. Well-designed brands communicate their core values through slogans, symbols, colors, and font types. Memorable brand names are distinctive and easy to remember. Strong brands own colors in their categories— UPS owns brown, Tiffany is clearly associated with its blue box, and Mary Kay's sales force are recognizable in their pink convertibles. Brand communication elements can also be used to keep a brand modern and relevant to its core constituency.

There is perhaps no more important asset to a firm than its strong, well-managed global brand. As John Stuart, the former CEO of Quaker Oats, once said, "If this business were split up, I would give you the land and bricks and I would take the brand and trademarks, and I would fare better than you."

Resources

Books

Aaker, David A. (2004). *Brand Portfolio Strategy: Creating Relevance, Differentiation, Energy, Leverage and Clarity*. Free Press.

Aaker, David A. (1996). *Building Strong Brands*. Free Press.

Aaker, David A., and Erich Joachimsthaler (2000). *Brand Leadership*. Free Press.

Gerzema, John, and Edward Le Bar (2008). *The Brand Bubble: The Looming Crisis in Brand Value and How to Avoid It*. Young & Rubicam Brands.

Keller, Kevin Lane (2012). *Building, Measuring, Managing Brand Equity* (4th edition). Pearson Prentice Hall.

Zaltman, Gerald, and Lindsay H. Zaltman (2008). *Marketing Metaphoria: What Deep Metaphors Reveal About the Minds of Consumers*. Harvard Business Press.

Articles

Aaker, David A. (2003). "The Power of the Branded Differentiator," *MIT Sloan Management Review*.

Aaker, David A., and Kevin Lane Keller (1990). "Consumer Evaluations of Brand Extensions." *Journal of Marketing* (January).

Aaker, Jennifer (1999). "The Malleable Self: The Role of Self-Expression in Persuasion. *Journal of Marketing Research*.

Aaker, Jennifer L., Veronica Benet-Martinez, and Jordi Garolera (2001). "A Study of Japanese and Spanish Brand Personality Constructs." *Journal of Personality and Social Psychology*.

Aaker, Jennifer, Susan Fournier, S. Adam Brasel (2004). "When Good Brands Do Bad." *Journal of Consumer Research* (June).

Ahluwalia, Rohini (2008). "How Far Can a Brand Stretch?" *Journal of Marketing Research* (June).

Fournier, Susan (1997). "Consumers and Their Brands: Developing Relationship Theory in Consumer Research." *Journal of Consumer Research*.

Fournier, Susan, and Lara Lee, (2009). "Getting Brand Communities Right." *Harvard Business Review* (March).

Holt, Douglas B., John A. Quelch, and Earl L. Taylor (2004). "How Global Brands Compete." *Harvard Business Review* (September).

Johar, Gita Venkataramani, Jaideep Sengupta, Jennifer Aaker (2005), "Two Roads to Updating Brand Personality Impressions: Trait versus Evaluative Inferencing." *Journal of Marketing Research* (November).

Keller, Kevin, Brian Sternthal, and Alice Tybout (2002). "Three Questions You Need to Ask About Your Brand." *Harvard Business Review.*

Lodish, Leonard M. and Carl F. Mela (2007). "If Brands are Built over Years, Why Are They Managed over Quarters?" *Harvard Business Review* (August).

Meyvis, Tom, Goldsmith, Kelly, Dhar, Ravi (2012), "The Importance of the Context in Brand Extension: How Pictures and Comparisons Shift Consumers' Focus from Fit to Quality," *Journal of Marketing Research* (April).

Muniz, Albert M. Jr., O'Guinn, Thomas C. (2001), "Brand Community," *Journal of Consumer Research* (March).

Roedder John, Deborah, Barbara Loken, Kyeongheui Kim, and Alokparna Basu Monga (2005). "Brand Concept Maps: A Methodology for Fortifying Brand Association Networks." *Marketing Science Institute Working Paper.*

Roedder John, Deborah, Barbara Loken, Kyeongheui Kim, and Alokparna Basu Monga (2006). "Brand Concept Maps: A Methodology for Identifying Brand Association Networks." *Journal of Marketing Research*, (November).

Rust, Roland T., Zeithaml, Valarie A., Lemon, Katherine N. (2004) "Customer-Centered Brand Management," *Harvard Business Review* (September), 110-118.

Sood, Sanjay, and Kevin Lane Keller (2012). "The Effects of Brand Name Structure on Brand Extension Evaluations and Parent Brand Dilution." *Journal of Marketing Research* (June). Sood, Sanjay, and Kevin Lane Keller. "Locus of Equity and Brand Extension." *Journal of Consumer Research* (March).

Wansink, Brian (2003). "Using Laddering to Understand Leverage a Brand's Equity." *Qualitative Market Research.*

Index

A

Aaker, David, 88–89
Aaker, Jennifer, 37
  brand personality dimensions, 39
Abercrombie & Fitch, 14
Absolut Vodka, 99
Adidas, 13
Aflac, 97
All State, 97
Amazon, 11
ambassadors for brands, 67
American Airlines, 19
Apple, 6, 12, 22, 33–34, 37, 55, 69, 73, 82, 86, 98
Armani, 73
AT&T, 12
attention grabbing, 13–15
attitudes to brand, 64–66
Audi A4, 89, 90
Autograph Collection of hotels, 80
awareness of brand, 62–64

B

Bath & Body Works, 30
BAV Consulting, 21–22, 74, 110
Benjamin Moore paints, 82
Ben & Jerry's ice cream, 12, 103
Best Buy, 11
Betty Crocker, 105
BMW, 11, 64–65
Bobbi Brown, 67
Body Shop, 30
Boston Market, 98
brand architecture, systems of brands
BrandAsset Valuator (BAV) model, 69, 74–78
  charts, 77–78
brand extension, 81, 82–83
  advantages and disadvantages of, 83–84
  fitting new product, 84–86

brand names, 95–96
  additional elements, 98–99
  color of logo, 99–100
  criteria in naming, 97–98
  translating into other languages, 97–98
brands. *See also* specific subject headings
brand architecture (*See* systems of brands)
  celebrities, use of, 100–102
  Coca-Cola controversy, 1–3
  extensions of brands (*See* brand extension)
  focus, product to customer, 4–5
  licensing of (*See* licensing of brands)
  management of (*See* management of brands)
  measurement of (*See* qualitative measurement; quantitative measurement)
  names (*See* brand names)
  ownership by customers, 6
  products distinguished from, 1–3
  purchase process, role in (*See* purchase process)
  repositioning brand (*See* repositioning brand)
  understanding brand equity, 6–8
  value of, 1–4, 94 (*See also* qualitative measurement; quantitative measurement)
Budweiser, 47–48
Buick, 89
Bulgari hotels, 79
Burberry, 20, 73, 85
Burger King, 105

C
Cadillac, 89
Calvin Klein, 14
Campbell's Soup Company, 2, 85
  rebuilding brand equity, 25–28
Candies, 87
Cathy, Dan, 103
celebrities, use of, 100–102
Chanel, 29, 34
Charlie the Tuna, 105
Cheerios, 81
Chevrolet, 89
China, 20–21
choices available, 9
Coach, 52, 69
Coca-Cola, 2, 19, 35, 37, 38,
  63, 69, 73, 97–98, 109
change of names, 2–3
  Diet Coke, 5
color of logo, 99–100
community around brand, 23
competition
  advantage or differentiation over,
    31–33
  identification of, 31
complaints about products, 24
Cool Whip, 91
Courtyard by Marriott, 79, 89,
  90, 91
Crayola, 82
Crest chewing gum, 33
Crest toothpaste, 89
customer-based brand evaluations,
  62
  attitudes to brand, 64–66
  attributes, choice of, 65–66
  awareness of brand, 62–64
  brand ambassadors-brand
    referral, 67
  diagnosing problems, 67–68
  loyalty to brand, 66–67

D
Dell Computers, 55
desire for right brand, 19–22
Deutsche Post World, 106–7
DHL, 106–7

Disney, 34, 89
Dunkin' Donuts, 6, 62, 98

E
emotional reactions to brands, 2–3,
  20–21
engagement with brand, 23–24
ESPN network, 81
Estée Lauder, 29–30, 31, 67, 95
ethnographic research, 47, 56–58
experience stage of purchasing, 22
  complaints or problems after
    purchase, 24
  relationships with brands, 22–24
extension of brand. See brand
  extension

F
Fab.com, 12
Facebook, 14, 16, 21, 22, 23,
  67, 95, 97
FarmVille, 23
Fast Company, 95
FedEx, 6, 12
Ferrari, 73
Ford, 95
French's mustard, 9, 16
Frito-Lay, 67

G
Gallo wines, 83
gamification, 23
Gap, 6
GE (General Electric), 37
Geico, 97
General Mills, 23, 81
General Motors, 89, 105
Germanotta, Stefani Joanne
  Angelina (Lady Gaga), 95–96
Gillette, 2
Gilt.com, 12
Gilt Groupe, 67
Giorgio Armani, 83
Goodrich, 97
Goodyear, 2, 97
Google, 19, 22, 73, 96
Green Giant, 23

H
Hallmark, 37
Harley-Davidson, 23, 73
Hastings, Reed, 45
Heinz ketchup, 99
Hillshire Farm, 81–82
Hill's Science Diet pet food, 12
Hush Puppies, 106

I
IBM, 6, 73
Iconix Brand Group, 87
Ikea, 19
Implicit Association Test (IAT),
    46–47, 53–56, 110
Intel, 6
Interbrand, 61, 69
    brand valuation model, 71–73
    interviews
    laddering interviews, 51–52
    messy data, 58–59
    ZMET interview, 50–51
iPad and iPod, 12, 82, 86
iTunes, 76
Ivory soap, 83, 89

J
JCPenney, 16
JCrew, 38
Jell-O pudding pops, 82
Joe Boxer, 87
Jones Apparel, 88
Juicy Fruit gum, 53
JW Marriott, 79

K
Kardashian, Kim, 100–101
Kellogg, 2
Kentucky Fried Chicken to KFC,
    98, 103
Kindle, 74
Kleenex, 19
Klout, 67
Kodak, 2, 104
Kohl's, 87
Kraft foods, 55, 91–92

L
laddering technique, 46, 51–53
Lady Gaga, 95–96, 100
Lady Goo Goo, 96
Lean Cuisine, 96
Levi Strauss, 37, 95

licensing of brands, 81–82
    advantages for licensee, 87
    benefits of, 86–87
    too much licensing, 86–87,
        87–88
Lipitor (drug), 55
Lipton, 2
logo and design elements, 98–100
Louis Vuitton, 20, 21
loyalty to brand, 66–67

M
MAC Cosmetics, 66, 67
McDonald's, 18–19, 37, 109
Macy's, 19, 38
Magla, 86
management of brands
    extension of brand, 81–86
        (*See* also brand extension)
    licensing, 86–88
Marriott example, 79–81
    positioning and communication
        strategies, 104–7
    protecting value, 94
    systems of brands (*See* systems
        of brands)
Mao suits, 20–21
market value/shareholder value,
    70–71
    BrandAsset Valuator (BAV)
        model, 69, 74–78
    Interbrand model, 71–73
Marlboro cigarettes, 34
Marriott Corporation, 79–81, 90,
    91, 95
Mary Kay cosmetics, 37, 100, 111
measurement of brands.
    See qualitative measurement;
    quantitative measurement

Mercedes-Benz, 37
mergers and acquisitions, 92–94
Michelin tires, 49, 95
Microsoft, 73
Miller High Life, 81–82
Miller Lite, 84
Mr. Clean, 86, 105
M&Ms, 82
monetary valuation of brand,
    68–69
    cost approaches, 69
    income approach, 70
Moshi Monsters, 96
MTV, 37
Muñiz, Albert, 23
mustard choices, 9

N
Nabisco, 2
names. See brand names
need for product
    attention, grabbing of, 13–15
    awareness of need, 11
    Campbell's Soup, 25–26
    high awareness of strong global
        brands, 12–13
    triggering need, 12
Neiman Marcus, 66–67
Nelson family (TV family), 3
Netflix, 45, 46
Nike, 13, 82, 96

O
Ogilvy, David, 109
O'Guinn, Tom, 23
Oldsmobile, 2
    repositioning effort, 104–5
Oreos, 85
Origins cosmetics, 29–30, 31,
    34–35, 42–43
Oscar Mayer, 91

P
Panasonic, 90
Pantene, 82–83
PeerIndex, 67
Pepsi Cola, 2, 35

Perry Ellis, 82
personalities of brands, 37–40
pharmaceutical detailing, 55
Philadelphia Cream Cheese, 91
Pinterest, 14
planning stage of purchasing,
    15–16
    clear images, strong brands, 19

    expectations, memory shaped by,
        16–17
    schemas of brand in memory,
        17–19, 26
Polo brand, 87–88
positioning strategy. See also
    repositioning brand
        advantage, relevant and
            desirable, 36–37
    Campbell's Soup, 25–28
    choices, making, 35–37
    competition, identification of
        and advantages over, 31–33
    disruptive positioning, 30
    Estée Lauder and Origins, 29–30,
        31, 34–35, 42–43
    experiential nature of, 37–40
    multisensory, emotional, social
        positioning, 39–42
    personalities of brands, 37–40
    targeting appropriately, 33–35
Pottery Barn, 82
price-quality inferences, 19–20
Proctor & Gamble (P&G), 86,
    89–90, 99
products distinguished from
    brands, 1–3
purchase process, 9–11. See also
    specific stages
    awareness of need, 11–15
    Campbell's reposition, 25–28
    creating interest, 15–19
    diagram of stages, 10
    experience stage, 22–24
    living stage, 11–15, 25–26
    planning stage, 15–19
    purchase and repurchase, 22–24
    shopping stage, 19–22, 26–27

Q
Quaker Oats, 111
qualitative measurement, 110
   data challenges, 58–59
   ethnographic research, 47, 56–58
   Implicit Association Test (IAT),
     46–47, 53–56
   laddering technique, 46, 51–53

   Zaltman metaphor elicitation
     technique (ZMET), 46, 47–51
quantitative measurement, 61–
   62, 110
   ambassadors for brands, 67
   attitudes to brand, 64–66
   awareness of brand, 62–64
   BrandAsset Valuator (BAV)
     model, 69, 74–78
   customer-based evaluations of
     brand effectiveness, 62–68
   dollar valuation of brand, 68–70
   guiding action using, 78 (See also
     management of brands)
   Interbrand model, 71–73
   loyalty to brand, 66–67
   market value/shareholder value,
     70–78
   problem diagnosis using data
     from, 67–68
   referrals for brands, 67
   Tobin's Q, 69
Qwikster, 45

R
Ralph Lauren, 85, 87–88, 95
recall of brand, unaided and aided,
   63
Reckitt Benckiser, 16
recognition of brand, 64
referrals for brands, 67
Renaissance Hotels, 80
Rent-A-Center, 61
Rent-a-Wreck, 96
repositioning brand
   Campbell's Soup Company,
     25–28
   dissonance and resolution, 104–5
   elements of brand used to

     communicate strategy, 106–7
   Oldsmobile example, 104–5
Revlon, 65
Ritz-Carlton hotels, 79, 80–81
RJ Reynolds, 95
RueLaLa.com, 12

S
Sara Lee Corporation, 81–83
schemas, 17–19
Sears, 87
segmentation of market, 5
semantic associative network,
   17–19
7-Eleven, 96
shareholder value. See market
   value/shareholder value
shopping stage, 19–20
   Campbell's reposition, 26–27
   emotional reactions to brands,
     20–21
   price-quality inferences, 19–20
   trust, importance of, 21–22
Smithsonian Museum, 99
Snapple, 12
Snickers, 82
Sony, 90
Southwest Airlines, 24
Sport Kit, 82
Springhill Suites, 79, 91
Starbucks, 6, 66, 73, 98
State Farm, 97
Stuart, John, 111
systems of brands, 82
   goals of, 88–89
   house of brands vs. branded
     house, 89–92
   mergers and acquisitions, 92–94
   shelf space, increase of, 90–91

T
Tabasco, 23
terminal values of products, 51–53
Tide, 89
Tiffany's, 100, 111
Timex, 37
Tinkertoys, 54
Tobin's Q, 69

TownPlace Suites, 79, 91
trust, importance of, 21–22
Twentieth Century Fox, 98
Twitalyzer, 67
Twitter, 21, 67, 95, 100

U
University of Illinois, 23
UPS, 100, 111

V
value of brand, 1–4. *See* also
    qualitative measurement;
    quantitative measurement
    protecting value, 94
values associated with products,
    51–53
Velveeta, 91
Verizon, 96
Virgin, 37, 89, 98
Visa, 19
Vodafone, 96
vodka brand, 49
Volkswagen, 96

W
Wade, Dwyane, 11
Wall Street Journal, 95
Walmart, 61, 96

Walton, Sam, 96
Warby Parker, 23
Warhol, Andy, 25
Weight Watchers, 85, 96
Westinghouse, 95
Winfrey, Oprah, 30
Woolworth's, 69, 95
WPP Group, 21, 74
Wrigley, 95

Y
Yale Locks, 95
Young & Rubicam, 110
BrandAsset Valuator (BAV) model,
    69, 74–78
Yves St. Laurent, 29

Z
Zaltman, Gerald, 46
Zaltman metaphor elicitation
    technique (ZMET), 46, 47–48,
    110
    levels of metaphors, 47–48
    universal deep metaphors, 48–49
ZMET interview, 50–51
Zappos, 14–15, 74
Zynga games, 23

About the Author

Barbara E. Kahn is the Patty and Jay H. Baker professor of Marketing and the director of the Jay H. Baker Retailing Center at the Wharton School at the University of Pennsylvania. Previously, Barbara served for three and a half years as the dean and Schein Family Chair professor of marketing at the School of Business Administration, University of Miami, Coral Gables, Florida. While dean at the University of Miami, she launched new global initiatives and academic programs, attracted top faculty from some of the world's leading business schools to enhance the caliber of the school's research and teaching, and established new partnerships with the business community. All of these initiatives helped the school rise significantly in the ratings. She also established the Global Business Forum at the University of Miami, which brought more than 1,000 leading business executives and professionals to the campus.

Before becoming dean at the University of Miami, Kahn spent 17 years at the Wharton School as the Dorothy Silberberg professor of marketing. She was also vice dean and director of the Wharton Undergraduate Program. She was a senior fellow of the Leonard Davis Institute and a faculty member of the Graduate Group in the Psychology Department. Before joining the Wharton faculty in 1990, Barbara served on the faculty at the Anderson School of Management at UCLA. She was the Hakuhodo Advertising Agency visiting scholar at the University of Tokyo in 1993 and a visiting academic at the University of Sydney, Australia, in 1996.

Kahn is an internationally recognized scholar on variety seeking, brand loyalty, retail assortment issues, and patient decision making. Her research provides marketing managers with a better understanding of the consumer choice process.

She has published more than 55 articles in leading academic journals. Between 1982 and 2006, she was the world's seventh-most-published author of articles in the most prestigious marketing journals. She coauthored *Grocery Revolution: The New Focus on the Consumer*, which chronicles the dramatically changing supermarket industry and outlines how consumers make choices within the supermarket.

Kahn has been elected president of the Association of Consumer Research and president of the *Journal of Consumer Research Policy* Board and was selected as a Marketing Science Institute trustee. She was also area editor at *Marketing Science* and associate editor at the *Journal of Consumer Research*. She is or has been on the editorial boards of the *Journal of Marketing Research, Marketing Science,* the *Journal of Marketing,* the *Journal of Consumer Research,* the *Journal of Behavioral Decision Making,* and *Marketing Letters*.

She received her PhD, MBA, and MPhil degrees from Columbia University, and a BA in English literature from the University of Rochester.

About the Wharton Executive Essentials Series

The *Wharton Executive Essentials* series from Wharton School Press brings the Wharton School's globally renowned faculty directly to you wherever you are. Inspired by Wharton's Executive Education program, each book is authored by a well-known expert and filled with real-life business examples and actionable advice. Available both as an ebook that is immediately downloadable to any e-reader and as a paperback edition sold through online retailers, each book offers a quick-reading, penetrating, and comprehensive summary of the knowledge that leaders need to excel in today's competitive business environment and capture tomorrow's opportunities.

WHARTON SCHOOL PRESS

About Wharton School Press

Wharton School Press, the book publishing arm of The Wharton School of the University of Pennsylvania, was established to inspire bold, insightful thinking within the global business community.

Wharton School Press publishes a select list of award-winning, bestselling, and thought-leading books that offer trusted business knowledge to help leaders at all levels meet the challenges of today and the opportunities of tomorrow. Led by a spirit of innovation and experimentation, Wharton School Press leverages groundbreaking digital technologies and has pioneered a fast-reading business book format that fits readers' busy lives, allowing them to swiftly emerge with the tools and information needed to make an impact. Wharton School Press books offer guidance and inspiration on a variety of topics, including leadership, management, strategy, innovation, entrepreneurship, finance, marketing, social impact, public policy, and more.

Wharton School Press also operates an online bookstore featuring a curated selection of influential books by Wharton School faculty and Press authors published by a wide range of leading publishers.

To find books that will inspire and empower you to increase your impact and expand your personal and professional horizons, visit *wsp.wharton.upenn.edu*.

About The Wharton School

Founded in 1881 as the world's first collegiate business school, the Wharton School of the University of Pennsylvania is shaping the future of business by incubating ideas, driving insights, and creating leaders who change the world. With a faculty of more than 235 renowned professors, Wharton has 5,000 undergraduate, MBA, Executive MBA, and doctoral students. Each year 18,000 professionals from around the world advance their careers through Wharton Executive Education's individual, company-customized, and online programs. More than 99,000 Wharton alumni form a powerful global network of leaders who transform business every day.

For more information, *visit www.wharton.upenn.edu.*

WHARTON ON MARKETING

\\
KNOWLEDGE FOR ACTION
//

When the media looks for experts to talk about current marketing trends, they turn to Wharton. Ours is the largest, most cited, and most published marketing faculty in the world.

Wharton's Marketing & Sales programs for executives offer the latest research and the best practices that deliver immediate impact to your organization and will give you a competitive edge.

Professor Barbara Kahn is the Faculty Director of **Brand Leadership: Strategies for Driving Growth in a Global Marketplace**.

WHARTON MARKETING & SALES PROGRAMS:

- **Bringing Customer Lifetime Value to Life**
- **Competitive Marketing Strategy**
- **Customer Driven Marketing (India)**
- **Leading the Effective Sales Force**
- **Pricing Strategies: Measuring, Capturing, and Retaining Value**
- **Strategic Marketing Essentials**
- **Wharton Marketing Metrics**™